WAITING FOR THE
BARBARIANS

J.M. Coetzee's work includes *Life & Times of Michael K*, *Boyhood: Scenes from Provincial Life*, *Youth*, *Elizabeth Costello* and *Disgrace*, which won the Booker Prize, making him the first author to have won it twice. In 2003 he was awarded the Nobel Prize for Literature.

ALSO BY J.M. COETZEE

Dusklands
In the Heart of the Country
Life & Times of Michael K
Foe
White Writing
Age of Iron
Doubling the Point: Essays and Interviews
The Master of Petersburg
Giving Offense
Boyhood: Scenes from Provincial Life
The Lives of Animals
Disgrace
Stranger Shores: Essays 1986–1999
Youth
Elizabeth Costello
Slow Man
Diary of a Bad Year
Summertime

J.M. Coetzee

WAITING FOR THE BARBARIANS

VINTAGE BOOKS
London

Published by Vintage 2004

17

Copyright © J.M. Coetzee 1980

J.M. Coetzee has asserted his right under the Copyright,
Designs and Patents Act 1988 to be identified as the author
of this work

First published in Great Britain in 1980 by
Secker & Warburg

First published by Vintage in 2000

Vintage
Random House, 20 Vauxhall Bridge Road,
London SW1V 2SA

www.vintage-books.co.uk

Addresses for companies within The Random House Group
Limited can be found at: www.randomhouse.co.uk/offices.htm

The Random House Group Limited Reg. No. 954009

A CIP catalogue record for this book
is available from the British Library

ISBN 9780099465935

The Random House Group Limited supports The Forest Stewardship
Council® (FSC®), the leading international forest-certification organisation.
Our books carrying the FSC label are printed on FSC®-certified paper. FSC is
the only forest-certification scheme supported by the leading environmental
organisations, including Greenpeace. Our paper procurement policy can be
found at www.randomhouse.co.uk/environment

Printed and bound by CPI Group (UK) Ltd, Croydon, CR0 4YY

For Nicolas and Gisela

I

I have never seen anything like it: two little discs of glass suspended in front of his eyes in loops of wire. Is he blind? I could understand it if he wanted to hide blind eyes. But he is not blind. The discs are dark, they look opaque from the outside, but he can see through them. He tells me they are a new invention. 'They protect one's eyes against the glare of the sun,' he says. 'You would find them useful out here in the desert. They save one from squinting all the time. One has fewer headaches. Look.' He touches the corners of his eyes lightly. 'No wrinkles.' He replaces the glasses. It is true. He has the skin of a younger man. 'At home everyone wears them.'

We sit in the best room of the inn with a flask between us and a bowl of nuts. We do not discuss the reason for his being here. He is here under the emergency powers, that is enough. Instead we talk about hunting. He tells me about the last great drive he rode in, when thousands of deer, pigs, bears were slain, so many that a mountain of carcases had to be left to rot ('Which was a pity'). I tell him about the great flocks of geese and ducks that descend on the lake every year in their migrations and about native ways of trapping them. I suggest that I take him out fishing by night in a native boat. 'That is an experience not to be missed,' I say; 'the fishermen carry flaming torches and beat drums over the water to drive the fish towards the nets they have laid.' He nods. He tells me about a visit he paid elsewhere on the frontier where people eat certain snakes as a delicacy, and about a huge antelope he shot.

He picks his way uncertainly among the strange furniture but does not remove the dark glasses. He retires early. He is quartered here at the inn because this is the best accommodation the town provides. I have impressed it on the staff that he is an important visitor. 'Colonel Joll is from the Third Bureau,' I tell them. 'The Third Bureau is the most important division of the Civil Guard nowadays.' That is what we hear, anyhow, in gossip that reaches us long out of date from the capital. The proprietor nods, the maids duck their heads. 'We must make a good impression on him.'

I carry my sleeping-mat out on to the ramparts where the night breeze gives some relief from the heat. On the flat roofs of the town I can make out by moonlight the shapes of other sleepers. From under the walnut trees on the square I still hear the murmur of conversation. In the darkness a pipe glows like a firefly, wanes, glows again. Summer is wheeling slowly towards its end. The orchards groan under their burden. I have not seen the capital since I was a young man.

I awake before dawn and tiptoe past the sleeping soldiers, who are stirring and sighing, dreaming of mothers and sweethearts, down the steps. From the sky thousands of stars look down on us. Truly we are here on the roof of the world. Waking in the night, in the open, one is dazzled.

The sentry at the gate sits cross-legged, fast asleep, cradling his musket. The porter's alcove is closed, his trolley stands outside. I pass.

'We do not have facilities for prisoners,' I explain. 'There is not much crime here and the penalty is usually a fine or compulsory labour. This hut is simply a storeroom attached to the granary, as you can see.' Inside it is close and smelly. There are no windows. The two prisoners lie bound on the floor. The smell comes from them, a smell of old urine. I call the guard in: 'Get these men to clean themselves, and please hurry.'

I show my visitor into the cool gloom of the granary itself. 'We hope for three thousand bushels from the communal land this year. We plant only once. The weather has been very kind to us.' We talk about rats and ways of controlling their numbers. When we return to the hut it smells of wet ash and the prisoners

2

are ready, kneeling in a corner. One is an old man, the other a boy. 'They were taken a few days ago,' I say. 'There was a raid not twenty miles from here. That is unusual. Normally they keep well away from the fort. These two were picked up afterwards. They say they had nothing to do with the raid. I do not know. Perhaps they are telling the truth. If you want to speak to them I will of course help with the language.'

The boy's face is puffy and bruised, one eye is swollen shut. I squat down before him and pat his cheek. 'Listen, boy,' I say in the patois of the frontier, 'we want to talk to you.'

He gives no response.

'He is pretending,' says the guard. 'He understands.'

'Who beat him?' I ask.

'It wasn't me,' he says. 'He was like that when he came.'

'Who beat you?' I ask the boy.

He is not listening to me. He stares over my shoulder, not at the guard but at Colonel Joll beside him.

I turn to Joll. 'He has probably never seen anything like it before.' I gesture. 'I mean the eyeglasses. He must think you are a blind man.' But Joll does not smile back. Before prisoners, it appears, one maintains a certain front.

I squat in front of the old man. 'Father, listen to me. We have brought you here because we caught you after a stock raid. You know that is a serious matter. You know you can be punished for it.'

His tongue comes out to moisten his lips. His face is grey and exhausted.

'Father, do you see this gentleman? This gentleman is visiting us from the capital. He visits all the forts along the frontier. His work is to find out the truth. That is all he does. He finds out the truth. If you do not speak to me you will have to speak to him. Do you understand?'

'Excellency,' he says. His voice croaks; he clears his throat. 'Excellency, we know nothing about thieving. The soldiers stopped us and tied us up. For nothing. We were on the road, coming here to see the doctor. This is my sister's boy. He has a sore that does not get better. We are not thieves. Show the Excellencies your sore.'

Nimbly, with hand and teeth, the boy begins unwrapping the rags that bandage his forearm. The last rounds, caked with blood and matter, stick to his flesh, but he lifts their edge to show me the red angry rim of the sore.

'You see,' the old man says, 'nothing will heal it. I was bringing him to the doctor when the soldiers stopped us. That is all.'

I walk back with my visitor across the square. Three women pass us, coming back from the irrigation dam with washbaskets on their heads. They eye us curiously, keeping their necks stiff. The sun beats down.

'These are the only prisoners we have taken for a long time,' I say. 'A coincidence: normally we would not have any barbarians at all to show you. This so-called banditry does not amount to much. They steal a few sheep or cut out a pack-animal from a train. Sometimes we raid them in return. They are mainly destitute tribespeople with tiny flocks of their own living along the river. It becomes a way of life. The old man says they were coming to see the doctor. Perhaps that is the truth. No one would have brought an old man and a sick boy along on a raiding party.'

I grow conscious that I am pleading for them.

'Of course one cannot be sure. But even if they are lying, how can they be of use to you, simple people like that?'

I try to subdue my irritation at his cryptic silences, at the paltry theatrical mystery of dark shields hiding healthy eyes. He walks with his hands clasped before him like a woman.

'Nevertheless,' he says, 'I ought to question them. This evening, if it is convenient. I will take my assistant along. Also I will need someone to help me with the language. The guard, perhaps. Does he speak it?'

'We can all make ourselves understood. You would prefer me not to be there?'

'You would find it tedious. We have set procedures we go through.'

*

4

Of the screaming which people afterwards claim to have heard from the granary, I hear nothing. At every moment that evening as I go about my business I am aware of what might be happening, and my ear is even tuned to the pitch of human pain. But the granary is a massive building with heavy doors and tiny windows; it lies beyond the abattoir and the mill in the south quarter. Also what was once an outpost and then a fort on the frontier has grown into an agricultural settlement, a town of three thousand souls in which the noise of life, the noise that all these souls make on a warm summer evening, does not cease because somewhere someone is crying. (At a certain point I begin to plead my own cause.)

When I see Colonel Joll again, when he has the leisure, I bring the conversation around to torture. 'What if your prisoner is telling the truth,' I ask, 'yet finds he is not believed? Is that not a terrible position? Imagine: to be prepared to yield, to yield, to have nothing more to yield, to be broken, yet to be pressed to yield more! And what a responsibility for the interrogator! How do you ever know when a man has told you the truth?'

'There is a certain tone,' Joll says. 'A certain tone enters the voice of a man who is telling the truth. Training and experience teach us to recognize that tone.'

'The tone of truth! Can you pick up this tone in everyday speech? Can you hear whether I am telling the truth?'

This is the most intimate moment we have yet had, which he brushes off with a little wave of the hand. 'No, you misunderstand me. I am speaking only of a special situation now, I am speaking of a situation in which I am probing for the truth, in which I have to exert pressure to find it. First I get lies, you see – this is what happens – first lies, then pressure, then more lies, then more pressure, then the break, then more pressure, then the truth. That is how you get the truth.'

Pain is truth; all else is subject to doubt. That is what I bear away from my conversation with Colonel Joll, whom with his tapering fingernails, his mauve handkerchiefs, his slender feet in soft shoes I keep imagining back in the capital he is so obviously impatient for, murmuring to his friends in theatre corridors between the acts.

(On the other hand, who am I to assert my distance from him? I drink with him, I eat with him, I show him the sights, I afford him every assistance as his letter of commission requests, and more. The Empire does not require that its servants love each other, merely that they perform their duty.)

The report he makes to me in my capacity as magistrate is brief.

'During the course of the interrogation contradictions became apparent in the prisoner's testimony. Confronted with these contradictions, the prisoner became enraged and attacked the investigating officer. A scuffle ensued during which the prisoner fell heavily against the wall. Efforts to revive him were unsuccessful.'

For the sake of completeness, as required by the letter of the law, I summon the guard and ask him to make a statement. He recites, and I take down his words: 'The prisoner became uncontrollable and attacked the visiting officer. I was called in to help subdue him. By the time I came in the struggle had ended. The prisoner was unconscious and bleeding from the nose.' I point to the place where he should make his mark. He takes the pen from me reverently.

'Did the officer tell you what to say to me?' I ask him softly.

'Yes, sir,' he says.

'Were the prisoner's hands tied?'

'Yes, sir. I mean, no, sir.'

I dismiss him and fill out the burial warrant.

But before I go to bed I take a lantern, cross the square, and circle through the back streets to the granary. There is a new guard at the door of the hut, another peasant boy wrapped in his blanket asleep. A cricket stops its singing at my approach. The pulling of the bolt does not waken the guard. I enter the hut holding the lantern high, trespassing, I realize, on what has become holy or unholy ground, if there is any difference, preserve of the mysteries of the State.

The boy lies on a bed of straw in a corner, alive, well. He seems to be sleeping, but the tension of his posture betrays him. His hands are tied in front of him. In the other corner is a long white bundle.

I wake the guard. 'Who told you to leave the body there? Who sewed it up?'

He hears the anger in my voice. 'It was the man who came with the other Excellency, sir. He was here when I came on duty. He said to the boy, I heard him, "Sleep with your grand-father, keep him warm." He pretended he was going to sew the boy into the shroud too, the same shroud, but he did not.'

While the boy still lies rigidly asleep, his eyes pinched shut, we carry the corpse out. In the yard, with the guard holding the lantern, I find the stitching with the point of my knife, tear the shroud open, and fold it back from the head of the old man.

The grey beard is caked with blood. The lips are crushed and drawn back, the teeth are broken. One eye is rolled back, the other eye-socket is a bloody hole. 'Close it up,' I say. The guard bunches the opening together. It falls open. 'They say that he hit his head on the wall. What do you think?' He looks at me warily. 'Fetch some twine and tie it shut.'

I hold the lantern over the boy. He has not stirred; but when I bend to touch his cheek he flinches and begins to tremble in long ripples that run up and down his body. 'Listen to me, boy,' I say, 'I am not going to harm you.' He rolls on his back and brings his bound hands up before his face. They are puffy and purple. I fumble at the bonds. All my gestures in relation to this boy are awkward. 'Listen: you must tell the officer the truth. That is all he wants to hear from you – the truth. Once he is sure you are telling the truth he will not hurt you. But you must tell him everything you know. You must answer every question he asks you truthfully. If there is pain, do not lose heart.' Picking at the knot I have at last loosened the rope. 'Rub your hands together till the blood begins to flow.' I chafe his hands between mine. He flexes his fingers painfully. I cannot pretend to be any better than a mother comforting a child between his father's spells of wrath. It has not escaped me that an interrogator can wear two masks, speak with two voices, one harsh, one seductive.

'Has he had anything to eat this evening?' I ask the guard.

'I do not know.'

'Have you had anything to eat?' I ask the boy. He shakes his head. I feel my heart grow heavy. I never wished to be drawn into this. Where it will end I do not know. I turn to the guard. 'I am leaving now, but there are three things I want you to do. First, when the boy's hands are better I want you to tie them again, but not so tightly that they swell. Second, I want you to leave the body where it is in the yard. Do not bring it back in. Early in the morning I will send a burial party to fetch it, and you will hand it over to them. If there are any questions, say I gave the orders. Third, I want you to lock the hut now and come with me. I will get you something from the kitchen for the boy to eat, which you will bring back. Come.'

I did not mean to get embroiled in this. I am a country magistrate, a responsible official in the service of the Empire, serving out my days on this lazy frontier, waiting to retire. I collect the tithes and taxes, administer the communal lands, see that the garrison is provided for, supervise the junior officers who are the only officers we have here, keep an eye on trade, preside over the law-court twice a week. For the rest I watch the sun rise and set, eat and sleep and am content. When I pass away I hope to merit three lines of small print in the Imperial gazette. I have not asked for more than a quiet life in quiet times.

But last year stories began to reach us from the capital of unrest among the barbarians. Traders travelling safe routes had been attacked and plundered. Stock thefts had increased in scale and audacity. A party of census officials had disappeared and been found buried in shallow graves. Shots had been fired at a provincial governor during a tour of inspection. There had been clashes with border patrols. The barbarian tribes were arming, the rumour went; the Empire should take pre-cautionary measures, for there would certainly be war.

Of this unrest I myself saw nothing. In private I observed that once in every generation, without fail, there is an episode of hysteria about the barbarians. There is no woman living along the frontier who has not dreamed of a dark barbarian hand coming from under the bed to grip her ankle, no man who has not frightened himself with visions of the barbarians carousing in his home, breaking the plates, setting fire to the curtains, raping his daughters. These dreams are the conse-quence of too much ease. Show me a barbarian army and I will believe.

In the capital the concern was that the barbarian tribes of the north and west might at last be uniting. Officers of the general staff were sent on tours of the frontier. Some of the garrisons were strengthened. Traders who requested them were given military escorts. And officials of the Third Bureau of the Civil Guard were seen for the first time on the frontier, guardians of the State, specialists in the obscurer motions of sedition, devotees of truth, doctors of interrogation. So now it seems my easy years are coming to an end, when I could sleep with a tranquil heart knowing that with a nudge here and a touch there the world would stay steady on its course. If I had only handed over these two absurd prisoners to the Colonel, I reflect – 'Here, Colonel, you are the specialist, see what you can make of them!' – if I had gone on a hunting trip for a few days, as I should have done, a visit up-river perhaps, and come back, and without reading it, or after skimming over it with an incurious eye, put my seal on his report, with no question about what the word *investigations* meant, what lay beneath it like a banshee beneath a stone – if I had done the wise thing, then perhaps I might now be able to return to my hunting and hawking and placid concupiscence while waiting for the provocations to cease and the tremors along the frontier to subside. But alas, I did not ride away: for a while I stopped my ears to the noises coming from the hut by the granary where

the tools are kept, then in the night I took a lantern and went
to see for myself.

From horizon to horizon the earth is white with snow. It falls
from a sky in which the source of light is diffuse and everywhere
present, as though the sun has dissolved into mist, become an
aura. In the dream I pass through the barracks gate, pass the
bare flagpole. The square extends before me, blending at its
edges into the luminous sky. Walls, trees, houses have dwindled,
lost their solidity, retired over the rim of the world.

As I glide across the square, dark figures separate out from
the whiteness, children at play building a snowcastle on top of
which they have planted a little red flag. They are mittened,
booted, muffled against the cold. Handful after handful of snow
they bring, plastering the walls of their castle, filling it out.
Their breath departs from them in white puffs. The rampart
around the castle is half built. I strain to pierce the queer floating
gabble of their voices but can make out nothing.

I am aware of my bulk, my shadowiness, therefore I am not
surprised that the children melt away on either side as I
approach. All but one. Older than the others, perhaps not even
a child, she sits in the snow with her hooded back to me
working at the door of the castle, her legs splayed, burrowing,
patting, moulding. I stand behind her and watch. She does not
turn. I try to imagine the face between the petals of her peaked
hood but cannot.

The boy lies on his back, naked, asleep, breathing fast and
shallow. His skin glistens with sweat. For the first time the
bandage is off his arm and I see the angry open sore it hid. I
bring the lantern closer. His belly and both groins are pocked
with little scabs and bruises and cuts, some marked by trickles
of blood.

'What did they do to him?' I whisper to the guard, the same
young man as last night.

'A knife,' he whispers back. 'Just a little knife, like this.' He spreads thumb and forefinger. Gripping his little knife of air he makes a curt thrust into the sleeping boy's body and turns the knife delicately, like a key, first left, then right. Then he withdraws it, his hand returns to his side, he stands waiting.

I kneel over the boy, bringing the light close to his face, and shake him. His eyes open languidly and close again. He sighs, his rapid breathing slows. 'Listen!' I say to him. 'You have been having a bad dream. You must wake up.' He opens his eyes and squints past the light at me.

The guard offers a pan of water. 'Can he sit?' I ask. The guard shakes his head. He raises the boy and helps him to sip.

'Listen,' I say. 'They tell me you have made a confession. They say you have admitted that you and the old man and other men from your clan have stolen sheep and horses. You have said that the men of your clan are arming themselves, that in the spring you are all going to join in a great war on the Empire. Are you telling the truth? Do you understand what this confession of yours will mean? Do you understand?' I pause; he looks back vacantly at all this vehemence, like someone tired after running a great distance. 'It means that the soldiers are going to ride out against your people. There is going to be killing. Kinsmen of yours are going to die, perhaps even your parents, your brothers and sisters. Do you really want that?' He makes no response. I shake his shoulder, slap his cheek. He does not flinch: it is like slapping dead flesh. 'I think he is very sick,' whispers the guard behind me, 'very sore and very sick.' The boy closes his eyes on me.

I call in the only doctor we have, an old man who earns his livelihood pulling teeth and making up aphrodisiacs out of bonemeal and lizards' blood. He puts a clay poultice on the sore and smears ointment on the hundred little stabs. Within a week, he promises, the boy will be able to walk. He recommends nourishing food and leaves in a hurry. He does not ask how the boy sustained his injuries.

But the Colonel is impatient. His plan is to launch a swift raid on the nomads and take more prisoners. He wants the boy along as a guide. He asks me to release thirty of the garrison of forty to him and to provide mounts.

I try to dissuade him. 'With no disrespect, Colonel,' I say, 'you are not a professional soldier, you have never had to campaign in these inhospitable parts. You will have no guide except a child who is terrified of you, who will say whatever comes into his head to please you, who is anyhow unfit to travel. You cannot rely on the soldiers to help you, they are only peasant conscripts, most of them have not been more than five miles from the settlement. The barbarians you are chasing will smell you coming and vanish into the desert while you are still a day's march away. They have lived here all their lives, they know the land. You and I are strangers – you even more than I. I earnestly advise you not to go.'

He hears me out, even (I have the feeling) leads me on a little. I am sure this conversation is noted down afterwards, with the comment that I am 'unsound'. When he has heard enough he dismisses my objections: 'I have a commission to fulfil, Magistrate. Only I can judge when my work is completed.' And he goes ahead with his preparations.

He travels in his black two-wheeled carriage, with camp-bed and folding writing-table strapped on the roof. I supply horses, carts, fodder and provisions for three weeks. A junior lieutenant of the garrison accompanies him. I speak to the lieutenant in private: 'Do not depend on your guide. He is weak and terrified. Keep an eye on the weather. Note landmarks. Your first duty is to bring our visitor back safely.' He bows.

I approach Joll again, trying to get an outline of his intentions.

'Yes,' he says. 'Of course I should not want to commit myself to a course beforehand. But, broadly speaking, we will locate the encampment of these nomads of yours and then proceed further as the situation dictates.'

'I ask,' I continue, 'only because if you get lost it becomes our task here to find you and bring you back to civilization.'

We pause, savouring from our different positions the ironies of the word.

'Yes, of course,' he says. 'But that is unlikely. We are fortunate to have the excellent maps of the region provided by yourself.'

'Those maps are based on little but hearsay, Colonel. I have patched them together from travellers' accounts over a period of ten or twenty years. I have never set foot myself where you plan to go. I am simply warning you.'

Since his second day here I have been too disturbed by his presence to be more than correct in my bearing towards him. I suppose that, like the roving headsman, he is used to being shunned. (Or is it only in the provinces that headsmen and torturers are still thought of as unclean?) Looking at him I wonder how he felt the very first time: did he, invited as an apprentice to twist the pincers or turn the screw or whatever it is they do, shudder even a little to know that at that instant he was trespassing into the forbidden? I find myself wondering too whether he has a private ritual of purification, carried out behind closed doors, to enable him to return and break bread with other men. Does he wash his hands very carefully, perhaps, or change all his clothes; or has the Bureau created new men who can pass without disquiet between the unclean and the clean?

Late into the night I hear the scraping and drumming of the orchestra under the old walnut trees across the square. There is a rosy glow in the air from the great bed of coals over which the soldiers are roasting whole sheep, a gift from the 'Excellency'. They will drink into the early hours, then set off at daybreak.

I find my way to the granary by the back alleys. The guard is not at his post, the door to the hut stands open. I am about to enter when I hear voices inside whispering and giggling.

I stare into pitch dark. 'Who is here?' I say.

There is a scrabbling sound and the young sentry stumbles against me. 'Sorry, sir,' he says. I smell his rum-sodden breath. 'The prisoner called me and I was trying to help him.' From the darkness comes a snort of laughter.

I sleep, wake to another round of dance-music from the square, fall asleep again, and dream of a body lying spread on its back, a wealth of pubic hair glistening liquid black and gold across the belly, up the loins, and down like an arrow into the furrow of the legs. When I stretch out a hand to brush the hair it begins to writhe. It is not hair but bees clustered densely atop one another: honey-drenched, sticky, they crawl out of the furrow and fan their wings.

My last act of courtesy is to ride out with the Colonel as far as where the road turns north-west along the coast of the lake. The sun is up and glares so savagely from the surface that I have to shield my eyes. The men, tired and queasy after their night of revels, straggle behind us. In the middle of the column, supported by a guard who rides side by side with him, comes the prisoner. His face is ghastly, he sits his horse uncomfortably, his wounds plainly still cause him pain. In the rear come the pack-horses and carts with water-casks, provisions, and the heavier equipment: lances, fusils, ammunition, tents. All in all not a stirring sight: the column rides raggedly, some of the men bareheaded, some wearing the heavy plumed cavalry helmet, others the simple leather cap. They avert their eyes from the glare, all save one, who looks sternly ahead through a strip of smoked glass glued to a stick which he holds up before his eyes in imitation of his leader. How far will this absurd affectation spread?

We ride in silence. The reapers, busy in the fields since before dawn, stop their work to wave as we pass. At the bend in the road I rein in and bid farewell. 'I wish you a safe return, Colonel,' I say. Framed in the window of his carriage he inclines his head inscrutably.

So I ride back, relieved of my burden and happy to be alone again in a world I know and understand. I climb the walls to watch the little column wind away along the north-west road towards the far green smudge where the river debouches into the lake and the line of vegetation vanishes into the haze of the desert. The sun still hangs bronze and heavy over the water. South of the lake stretch marshlands and salt flats, and beyond them a blue-grey line of barren hills. In the fields the farmers are loading the two huge old hay-wagons. A flight of mallard wheels overhead and glides down towards the water. Late summer, a time of peace and plenty. I believe in peace, perhaps even peace at any price.

Two miles due south of the town a cluster of dunes stands out from the flat sandy landscape. Catching frogs in the marshes and coasting down the slopes of the dunes on polished wooden sleds are the staple summer sports of the children, the one for the mornings, the other for the evenings when the sun goes down and the sand begins to cool. Though the wind blows at all seasons, the dunes are stable, being held together by a cap of thin grass and also, as I found by accident a few years ago, by timber skeletons. For the dunes cover the ruins of houses that date back to times long before the western provinces were annexed and the fort was built.

One of my hobbies has been to excavate these ruins. If there are no repairs to be done to the irrigation works, I sentence petty offenders to a few days of digging in the dunes; soldiers are sent here on punishment details; and at the height of my enthusiasm I even used to pay for casual labour out of my own pocket. The work is unpopular, for the diggers must toil under a hot sun or in a biting wind with no shelter and with sand flying everywhere. They work half-heartedly, not sharing my interest (which they see as whimsical), discouraged by the speed at which the sand drifts back. But in the course of a few years I have succeeded in uncovering several of the largest structures to floor level. The most recently excavated stands out like a shipwreck in the desert, visible even from the town walls. From this structure, perhaps a public building or a temple, I have recovered the heavy poplar lintel, carved with a design of interlaced leaping fish, that now hangs over my fireplace. Buried below floor level in a bag that crumbled to nothing as soon as it was touched I also found a cache of wooden slips on which are painted characters in a script I have not seen the like of.

We have found slips like these before, scattered like clothespegs in the ruins, but most so bleached by the action of sand that the writing has been illegible. The characters on the new slips are as clear as the day they were written. Now, in the hope of deciphering the script, I have set about collecting all the slips I can, and have let the children who play here know that if they find one it is always worth a penny.

The timbers we uncover are dry and powdery. Many have been held together only by the surrounding sand and, once exposed, crumble. Others snap off at the lightest pressure. How old the wood is I do not know. The barbarians, who are pastoralists, nomads, tent-dwellers, make no reference in their legends to a permanent settlement near the lake. There are no human remains among the ruins. If there is a cemetery we have not found it. The houses contain no furniture. In a heap of ashes I have found fragments of sun-dried clay pottery and something brown which may once have been a leather shoe or cap but which fell to pieces before my eyes. I do not know where the wood came from to build these houses. Perhaps in bygone days criminals, slaves, soldiers trekked the twelve miles to the river, and cut down poplar trees, and sawed and planed them, and transported the timbers back to this barren place in carts, and built houses, and a fort too, for all I know, and in the course of time died, so that their masters, their prefects and magistrates and captains, could climb the roofs and towers morning and evening to scan the world from horizon to horizon for signs of the barbarians. Perhaps in my digging I have only scratched the surface. Perhaps ten feet below the floor lie the ruins of another fort, razed by the barbarians, peopled with the bones of folk who thought they would find safety behind high walls. Perhaps when I stand on the floor of the courthouse, if that is what it is, I stand over the head of a magistrate like myself, another grey-haired servant of Empire who fell in the arena of his authority, face to face at last with the barbarian. How will I ever know? By burrowing like a rabbit? Will the characters on the slips one day tell me? There were two hundred and fifty-six slips in the bag. Is it by chance that the number is perfect? After I had first counted them and made this discovery I cleared the floor of my office and laid them out, first in one great square, then in sixteen smaller squares, then in other combinations, thinking that what I had hitherto taken to be characters in a syllabary might in fact be elements of a picture whose outline would leap at me if I struck on the right arrangement: a map of the land of the barbarians in olden times, or a representation of a lost pantheon. I have even found myself reading the slips in a mirror, or tracing one on top of another, or conflating half of one with half of another.

One evening I lingered among the ruins after the children had run home to their suppers, into the violet of dusk and the first stars, the hour when, according to lore, ghosts awaken. I put my ear to the ground as the children had instructed me, to hear what they hear: thumps and groans under the earth, the deep irregular beating of drums. Against my cheek I felt the patter of sand driving from nowhere to nowhere across the wastes. The last light faded, the ramparts grew dim against the sky and dissolved into the darkness. For an hour I waited, wrapped in my cloak, with my back against the corner-post of a house in which people must once have talked and eaten and played music. I sat watching the moon rise, opening my senses to the night, waiting for a sign that what lay around me, what lay beneath my feet, was not only sand, the dust of bones, flakes of rust, shards, ash. The sign did not come. I felt no tremor of ghostly fear. My nest in the sand was warm. Before long I caught myself nodding.

I stood up and stretched; then I trudged home through the balmy darkness, taking my bearings from the dim sky-glow of the household fires. Ridiculous, I thought: a greybeard sitting in the dark waiting for spirits from the byways of history to speak to him before he goes home to his military stew and his comfortable bed. The space about us here is merely space, no meaner or grander than the space above the shacks and ten- ements and temples and offices of the capital. Space is space, life is life, everywhere the same. But as for me, sustained by the toil of others, lacking civilized vices with which to fill my

leisure, I pamper my melancholy and try to find in the vacuous-
ness of the desert a special historical poignancy. Vain, idle,
misguided! How fortunate that no one sees me!

Today, only four days after the departure of the expedition, the
first of the Colonel's prisoners arrive. From my window I watch
them cross the square between their mounted guards, dusty,
exhausted, cringing already from the spectators who crowd
about them, the skipping children, the barking dogs. In the
shade of the barracks wall the guards dismount; at once
the prisoners squat down to rest, save for a little boy who stands
on one leg, his arm on his mother's shoulder, staring back
curiously at the onlookers. Someone brings a bucket of water
and a ladle. They drink thirstily, while the crowd grows and
presses in so tight around them that I can no longer see.
Impatiently I wait for the guard who now pushes his way
through the crowd and crosses the barracks yard.

'How do you explain this?' I shout at him. He bows his
head, fumbles at his pockets. 'These are fishing people! How
can you bring them back here?'

He holds out a letter. I break the seal and read: 'Please hold
these and succeeding detainees incommunicado for my return.'
Beneath his signature the seal is repeated, the seal of the Bureau
which he has carried with him into the desert and which, if
he perished, I would doubtless have to send out a second
expedition to recover.

'The man is ridiculous!' I shout. I storm about the room.
One should never disparage officers in front of men, fathers in
front of children, but towards this man I discover no loyalty
in my heart. 'Did no one tell him these are fishing people? It
is a waste of time bringing them here! You are supposed to
help him track down thieves, bandits, invaders of the Empire!
Do these people look like a danger to the Empire?' I fling the
letter at the window.

The crowd parts before me till I stand at the centre con-
fronting the dozen pathetic prisoners. They flinch before my

anger, the little boy sliding into his mother's arms. I gesture to the guards: 'Clear a way and bring these people into the barracks yard!' They herd the captives along; the barracks gate closes behind us. 'Now explain yourselves,' I say; 'did no one tell him these prisoners are useless to him? Did no one tell him the difference between fishermen with nets and wild nomad horsemen with bows? Did no one tell him they don't even speak the same language?'

One of the soldiers explains. 'When they saw us coming they tried to hide in the reeds. They saw horsemen coming so they tried to hide. So the officer, the Excellency, ordered us to take them in. Because they were hiding.'

I could curse with vexation. A policeman! The reasoning of a policeman! 'Did the Excellency say why he wanted them brought back here? Did he say why he could not ask them his questions out there?'

'None of us could speak their language, sir.'

Of course not! These river people are aboriginal, older even than the nomads. They live in settlements of two or three families along the banks of the river, fishing and trapping for most of the year, paddling to the remote southern shores of the lake in the autumn to catch redworms and dry them, building flimsy reed shelters, groaning with cold through the winter, dressing in skins. Living in fear of everyone, skulking in the reeds, what can they possibly know of a great barbarian enterprise against the Empire?

I send one of the men to the kitchen for food. He comes back with a loaf of yesterday's bread which he offers to the oldest prisoner. The old man accepts the bread reverentially in both hands, sniffs it, breaks it, passes the lumps around. They stuff their mouths with this manna, chewing fast, not raising their eyes. A woman spits masticated bread into her palm and feeds her baby. I motion for more bread. We stand watching them eat as though they are strange animals.

'Let them stay in the yard,' I tell their guards. 'It will be inconvenient for us, but there is nowhere else. If it gets cold tonight I will make another arrangement. See that they are fed.

Give them something to do to keep their hands busy. Keep the gate closed. They will not run away but I do not want idlers coming in to stare at them.'

So I check my anger and do as the Colonel instructs: I hold his useless prisoners 'incommunicado' for him. And in a day or two these savages seem to forget they ever had another home. Seduced utterly by the free and plentiful food, above all by the bread, they relax, smile at everyone, move about the barracks yard from one patch of shade to another, doze and wake, grow excited as mealtimes approach. Their habits are frank and filthy. One corner of the yard has become a latrine where men and women squat openly and where a cloud of flies buzzes all day. ('Give them a spade!' I tell the guards; but they do not use it.) The little boy, grown quite fearless, haunts the kitchen, begging sugar from the maids. Aside from bread, sugar and tea are great novelties to them. Every morning they get a small block of pressed tea-leaves which they boil up in a four-gallon pail on a tripod over a fire. They are happy here; indeed unless we chase them away they may stay with us forever, so little does it seem to have taken to lure them out of a state of nature. I spend hours watching them from the upstairs window (other idlers have to watch through the gate). I watch the women picking lice, combing and plaiting each other's long black hair. Some of them have fits of harsh dry coughing. It is striking that there are no children in the group but the baby and the little boy. Did some of them, the nimble, the wakeful, after all succeed in escaping from the soldiers? I hope so. I hope that when we return them to their homes along the river they will have many far-fetched stories to tell their neighbours. I hope that the history of their captivity enters their legends, passed down from grandfather to grandson. But I hope too that memories of the town, with its easy life and its exotic foods, are not strong enough to lure them back. I do not want a race of beggars on my hands.

For a few days the fisherfolk are a diversion, with their strange gabbling, their vast appetites, their animal shamelessness, their volatile tempers. The soldiers lounge in the doorways watching them, making obscene comments about them which they do not understand, laughing; there are always children with their faces pressed to the bars of the gate; and from my window I stare down, invisible behind the glass.

Then, all together, we lose sympathy with them. The filth, the smell, the noise of their quarrelling and coughing become too much. There is an ugly incident when a soldier tries to drag one of their women indoors, perhaps only in play, who knows, and is pelted with stones. A rumour begins to go the rounds that they are diseased, that they will bring an epidemic to the town. Though I make them dig a pit in the corner of the yard and have the nightsoil removed, the kitchen staff refuse them utensils and begin to toss them their food from the doorway as if they were indeed animals. The soldiers lock the door to the barracks hall, the children no longer come to the gate. Someone flings a dead cat over the wall during the night and causes an uproar. Through the long hot days they moon about the empty yard. The baby cries and coughs, cries and coughs till I flee for refuge to the farthest corner of my appartment. I write an angry letter to the Third Bureau, unsleeping guardian of the Empire, denouncing the incompetence of one of its agents. 'Why do you not send people with experience of the frontier to investigate frontier unrest?' I write. Wisely I tear up the letter. If I unlock the gate in the dead of night, I wonder, will the fisherfolk sneak away? But I do nothing. Then one day I notice that the baby has stopped crying. When I look from the window it is nowhere to be seen. I send a guard to search and he finds the little corpse under its mother's clothes. She will not yield it up, we have to tear it away from her. After this she squats alone all day with her face covered, refusing to eat. Her people seem to shun her. Have we violated some custom of theirs, I wonder, by taking the child and burying it? I curse Colonel Joll for all the trouble he has brought me, and for the shame too.

Then in the middle of the night he is back. Bugle-calls from the ramparts break into my sleep, the barracks hall erupts in uproar as the soldiers go scrambling for their weapons. My head is confused, I am slow in dressing, by the time I emerge on to the square the column is already passing through the gates, some of the men riding, some leading their mounts. I stand back while the onlookers crowd around, touching and embracing the soldiers, laughing with excitement ('All safe!' someone shouts), until coming up in the middle of the column I see what I have been dreading: the black carriage, then the shuffling group of prisoners roped together neck to neck, shapeless figures in their sheepskin coats under the silver moonlight, then behind them the last of the soldiers leading the carts and pack-horses. As more and more people come running up, some with flaming torches, and the babble mounts, I turn my back on the Colonel's triumph and make my way back to my rooms. This is the point at which I begin to see the disadvantages of living, as I have chosen to do, in the rambling apartment over the storerooms and kitchen intended for the military commandant we have not had for years, rather than in the attractive villa with geraniums in the windows which falls to the lot of the civil magistrate. I would like to be able to stop my ears to the noises coming from the yard below, which has now, it appears, become permanently a prison yard. I feel old and tired, I want to sleep. I sleep whenever I can nowadays and, when I wake up, wake reluctantly. Sleep is no longer a healing bath, a recuperation of vital forces, but an oblivion, a nightly brush with annihilation. Living in the apartment has become bad for me, I think; but not only that. If I lived in the magistrate's villa on the quietest street in town, holding sittings of the court on Mondays and Thursdays, going hunting every morning, occupying my evenings in the classics, closing my ears to the activities of this upstart policeman, if I resolved to ride out the bad times, keeping my own counsel, I might cease to feel like a man who, in the grip of the undertow, gives up the fight, stops swimming, and turns his face towards the open sea and death. But it is the knowledge of how contingent my unease is, how dependent on a baby that wails beneath my window one day and does not wail the next, that brings the worst shame to me, the greatest indifference to annihilation. I know somewhat too much; and from this knowledge, once one has been infected, there seems to be no recovering. I ought never to have taken my lantern to see what was going on in the hut by the granary. On the other hand, there was no way, once I had picked up the lantern, for me to put it down again. The knot loops in upon itself; I cannot find the end.

All the next day the Colonel spends sleeping in his room at the inn, and the staff have to tiptoe about their duties. I try to pay no attention to the new batch of prisoners in the yard. It is a pity that all the doors of the barracks block as well as the stairway leading up to my apartment open on to the yard. I hurry out in the early-morning light, occupy myself all day with municipal rents, dine in the evening with friends. On the way home I meet the young lieutenant who accompanied Colonel Joll into the desert and congratulate him on his safe return. 'But why did you not explain to the Colonel that the fishing people could not possibly help him in his inquiries?' He looks embarrassed. 'I spoke to him,' he tells me, 'but all he said was, "Prisoners are prisoners". I decided it was not my place to argue with him.'

The next day the Colonel begins his interrogations. Once I thought him lazy, little more than a bureaucrat with vicious tastes. Now I see how mistaken I was. In his quest for the truth he is tireless. The questioning starts in the early morning and is still going on when I return after dark. He has enlisted the aid of a hunter who has shot pigs up and down the river all his life and knows a hundred words of the fisherfolk's language. One by one the fisherfolk are taken into the room where the Colonel has established himself, to be asked whether they have seen movements of strange horsemen. Even the child is questioned: 'Have strangers visited your father during the night?' (I guess, of course, at what passes in that room, at the fear, the bewilderment, the abasement.) The prisoners are returned not to the yard but to the main barracks hall: the soldiers have been turned out, quartered on the town. I sit in my rooms with the windows shut, in the stifling warmth of a windless evening, trying to read, straining my ears to hear or not to hear sounds of violence. Finally at midnight the interrogations cease, there is no more banging of doors or tramping of feet, the yard is silent in the moonlight, and I am at liberty to sleep.

The joy has gone from my life. I spend the day playing with lists and numbers, stretching petty tasks to fill the hours. In the evening I eat at the inn; then, reluctant to go home, make my way upstairs to the warren of cubicles and partitioned rooms where the ostlers sleep and the girls entertain men-friends.

I sleep like a dead man. When I wake up in the thin early-morning light the girl is lying curled up on the floor. I touch her arm: 'Why are you sleeping there?'

She smiles back. 'It is all right. I am quite comfortable.' (That is true: lying on the soft sheepskin rug she stretches and yawns, her neat little body not even filling it.) 'You were tossing in your sleep, you told me to go away, so I decided I would sleep better here.'

'I told you to go away?'

'Yes: in your sleep. Don't be upset.' She climbs into bed beside me. I embrace her with gratitude, without desire.

'I would like to sleep here again tonight,' I say. She nuzzles my chest. It occurs to me that whatever I want to say to her will be heard with sympathy, with kindness. But what can I possibly say? 'Terrible things go on in the night while you and I are asleep'? The jackal rips out the hare's bowels, but the world rolls on.

Another day and another night I spend away from the empire of pain. I fall asleep in the girl's arms. In the morning she is again lying on the floor. She laughs at my dismay: 'You pushed me out with your hands and feet. Please don't get upset. We cannot help our dreams or what we do in our sleep.' I groan and turn my face away. I have known her a year, visiting her sometimes twice a week in this room. I feel a quiet affection for her which is perhaps the best that can be hoped for between an aging man and a girl of twenty; better than a possessive passion certainly. I have played with the idea of asking her to live with me. I try to remember by what nightmare I am possessed when I push her away, but fail. 'If I ever do it again you must promise to wake me,' I tell her.

Then, in my office at the courthouse, a visitor is announced. Colonel Joll, wearing his dark eyeshades indoors, enters and sits down opposite me. I offer him tea, surprised at how steady my hand is. He is leaving, he says. Should I try to conceal my joy? He sips his tea, sitting carefully upright, inspecting the room, the shelves upon shelves of papers bundled together and tied with ribbon, the record of decades of humdrum administration, the small bookcase of legal texts, the cluttered desk. He has completed his inquiries for the time being, he says, and is in a hurry to return to the capital and make his report. He has an air of sternly controlled triumph. I nod my understanding. 'Anything that I can do to facilitate your journey . . .' I say. There is a pause. Then into the silence, like a pebble into a pool, I drop my question.

'And your inquiries, Colonel, among the nomad peoples and the aboriginals – have they been as successful as you wished?'

He places his fingers together tip to tip before he answers. I have the feeling that he knows how much his affectations irritate me. 'Yes, Magistrate, I can say that we have had some success. Particularly when you consider that similar investigations are being carried out elsewhere along the frontier in a co-ordinated fashion.'

'That is good. And can you tell us whether we have anything to fear? Can we rest securely at night?'

The corner of his mouth crinkles in a little smile. Then he stands up, bows, turns, and leaves. Early next morning he departs accompanied by his small escort, taking the long east road back to the capital. Throughout a trying period he and I have managed to behave towards each other like civilized people. All my life I have believed in civilized behaviour; on this occasion, however, I cannot deny it, the memory leaves me sick with myself.

My first action is to visit the prisoners. I unlock the barracks hall which has been their jail, my senses already revolting at the sickly smell of sweat and ordure, and throw the doors wide open. 'Get them out of there!' I shout at the half-dressed soldiers who stand about watching me as they eat their porridge. From the gloom inside the prisoners stare apathetically back. 'Go in there and clean up that room!' I shout. 'I want everything cleaned up! Soap and water! I want everything as it was before!' The soldiers hurry to obey; but why is my anger directed at them, they must be asking. Into the daylight emerge the prisoners, blinking, shielding their eyes. One of the women has to be helped. She shakes all the time like an old person, though she is young. There are some too sick to stand up.

I last saw them five days ago (if I can claim ever to have seen them, if I ever did more than pass my gaze over their surface absently, with reluctance). What they have undergone in these five days I do not know. Now herded by their guards they stand in a hopeless little knot in the corner of the yard, nomads and fisherfolk together, sick, famished, damaged, terrified. It would be best if this obscure chapter in the history of the world were terminated at once, if these ugly people were obliterated from the face of the earth and we swore to make a new start, to run an empire in which there would be no more injustice, no more pain. It would cost little to march them out into the desert (having put a meal in them first, perhaps, to make the march possible), to have them dig, with their last strength, a pit large enough for all of them to lie in (or even to dig it for them!), and, leaving them buried there forever and forever, to come back to the walled town full of new intentions, new resolutions. But that will not be my way. The new men of Empire are the ones who believe in fresh starts, new chapters, clean pages; I struggle on with the old story, hoping that before it is finished it will reveal to me why it was that I thought it worth the trouble. Thus it is that, administration of law and order in these parts having today passed back to me, I order that the prisoners be fed, that the doctor be called in to do what he can, that the barracks return to being a barracks, that arrangements be made to restore the prisoners to their former lives as soon as possible, as far as possible.

II

She kneels in the shade of the barracks wall a few yards from the gate, muffled in a coat too large for her, a fur cap open before her on the ground. She has the straight black eyebrows, the glossy black hair of the barbarians. What is a barbarian woman doing in town begging? There are no more than a few pennies in the cap.

Twice more during the day I pass her. Each time she gives me a strange regard, staring straight ahead of her until I am near, then very slowly turning her head away from me. The second time I drop a coin into the cap. 'It is cold and late to be outdoors,' I say. She nods. The sun is setting behind a strip of black cloud; the wind from the north already carries a hint of snow; the square is empty; I pass on.

The next day she is not there. I speak to the gatekeeper: 'There was a woman sitting over there all of yesterday, begging. Where does she come from?' The woman is blind, he replies. She is one of the barbarians the Colonel brought in. She was left behind.

A few days later I see her crossing the square, walking slowly and awkwardly with two sticks, the sheepskin coat trailing behind her in the dust. I give orders; she is brought to my rooms, where she stands before me propped on her sticks. 'Take off your cap,' I say. The soldier who has brought her in lifts off the cap. It is the same girl, the same black hair cut in a fringe across the forehead, the same broad mouth, the black eyes that look through and past me.

'They tell me you are blind.'

'I can see,' she says. Her eyes move from my face and settle somewhere behind me to my right.

27

'Where do you come from?' Without thinking I cast a glance over my shoulder: she is staring at nothing but empty wall. Her gaze has grown rigid. Already knowing the answer, I repeat my question. She meets it with silence.

I dismiss the soldier. We are alone.

'I know who you are,' I say. 'Will you please sit?' I take her sticks and help to seat her on a stool. Under the coat she wears wide linen drawers tucked into heavy-soled boots. She smells of smoke, of stale clothing, of fish. Her hands are horny.

'Do you make a living by begging?' I ask. 'You know you are not supposed to be in town. We could expel you at any time and send you back to your people.'

She sits staring eerily ahead of her.

'Look at me,' I say.

'I am looking. This is how I look.'

I wave a hand in front of her eyes. She blinks. I bring my face closer and stare into her eyes. She wheels her gaze from the wall on to me. The black irises are set off by milky whites as clear as a child's. I touch her cheek: she starts.

'I asked how you make a living.'

She shrugs. 'I do washing.'

'Where do you live?'

'I live.'

'We do not permit vagrants in the town. Winter is almost here. You must have somewhere to live. Otherwise you must go back to your own people.'

She sits obdurately. I know I am beating about the bush.

'I can offer you work. I need someone to keep these rooms tidy, to see to my laundry. The woman who does it at present is not satisfactory.'

She understands what I am offering. She sits very stiff, her hands in her lap.

'Are you alone? Please answer.'

'Yes.' Her voice comes in a whisper. She clears her throat. 'Yes.'

'I have offered that you should come and work here. You cannot beg in the streets. I cannot permit that. Also you must have a place of abode. If you work here you can share the cook's room.'

'You do not understand. You do not want someone like me.' She gropes for her sticks. I know that she cannot see. 'I am . . .' – she holds up her forefinger, grips it, twists it. I have no idea what the gesture means. 'Can I go?' She makes her own way to the head of the stairs, then has to wait for me to help her down.

A day passes. I stare out over the square where the wind chases flurries of dust. Two little boys are playing with a hoop. They bowl it into the wind. It rolls forward, slows, teeters, rides back, falls. The boys lift their faces and run after it, the hair whipped back from their clean brows.

I find the girl and stand before her. She sits with her back against the trunk of one of the great walnut trees: it is hard to see whether she is even awake. 'Come,' I say, and touch her shoulder. She shakes her head. 'Come,' I say, 'everyone is indoors.' I beat the dust from her cap and hand it to her, help her to her feet, walk slowly beside her across the square, empty now save for the gatekeeper, who shades his eyes to stare at us.

The fire is lit. I draw the curtains, light the lamp. She refuses the stool, but yields up her sticks and kneels in the centre of the carpet.

'This is not what you think it is,' I say. The words come reluctantly. Can I really be about to excuse myself? Her lips are clenched shut, her ears too no doubt, she wants nothing of old men and their bleating consciences. I prowl around her, talking about our vagrancy ordinances, sick at myself. Her skin begins to glow in the warmth of the closed room. She tugs at her coat, opens her throat to the fire. The distance between myself and her torturers, I realize, is negligible; I shudder.

'Show me your feet,' I say in the new thick voice that seems to be mine. 'Show me what they have done to your feet.'

She neither helps nor hinders me. I work at the thongs and eyelets of the coat, throw it open, pull the boots off. They are a man's boots, far too large for her. Inside them her feet are swaddled, shapeless.

'Let me see,' I say.

She begins to unwrap the dirty bandages. I leave the room, go downstairs to the kitchen, come back with a basin and a pitcher of warm water. She sits waiting on the carpet, her feet bare. They are broad, the toes stubby, the nails crusted with dirt.

She runs a finger across the outside of her ankle. 'That is where it was broken. The other one too.' She leans back on her hands and stretches her legs.

'Does it hurt?' I say. I pass my finger along the line, feeling nothing.

'Not any more. It has healed. But perhaps when the cold comes.'

'You should sit,' I say. I help her off with the coat, seat her on the stool, pour the water into the basin, and begin to wash her feet. For a while her legs remain tense; then they relax.

I wash slowly, working up a lather, gripping her firm-fleshed calves, manipulating the bones and tendons of her feet, running my fingers between her toes. I change my position to kneel not in front of her but beside her, so that, holding a leg between elbow and side, I can caress the foot with both hands.

I lose myself in the rhythm of what I am doing. I lose awareness of the girl herself. There is a space of time which is blank to me: perhaps I am not even present. When I come to, my fingers have slackened, the foot rests in the basin, my head droops.

I dry the right foot, shuffle to the other side, lift the leg of the wide drawers above her knee, and, fighting against drowsiness, begin to wash the left foot. 'Sometimes this room gets very hot,' I say. The pressure of her leg against my side does not lessen. I go on. 'I will find clean bandages for your feet,' I say, 'but not now.' I push the basin aside and dry the foot. I am aware of the girl struggling to stand up; but now, I think, she must take care of herself. My eyes close. It becomes an intense pleasure to keep them closed, to savour the blissful giddiness. I stretch out on the carpet. In an instant I am asleep. In the middle of the night I wake up cold and stiff. The fire is out, the girl is gone.

I watch her eat. She eats like a blind person, gazing into the distance, working by touch. She has a good appetite, the appetite of a robust young countrywoman.

'I don't believe you can see,' I say.

'Yes, I can see. When I look straight there is nothing, there is − ' (she rubs the air in front of her like someone cleaning a window).

'A blur,' I say.

'There is a blur. But I can see out of the sides of my eyes. The left eye is better than the right. How could I find my way if I didn't see?'

'Did they do it to you?'

'Yes.'

'What did they do?'

She shrugs and is silent. Her plate is empty. I dish up more of the bean stew she seems to like so much. She eats too fast, belches behind a cupped hand, smiles. 'Beans make you fart,' she says. The room is warm, her coat hangs in a corner with the boots below it, she wears only the white smock and drawers. When she does not look at me I am a grey form moving about unpredictably on the periphery of her vision. When she looks at me I am a blur, a voice, a smell, a centre of energy that one day falls asleep washing her feet and the next day feeds her bean stew and the next day − she does not know.

I seat her, fill the basin, roll the drawers above her knees. Now that the two feet are together in the water I can see that the left is turned further inward than the right, that when she stands she must stand on the outer edges of her feet. Her ankles are large, puffy, shapeless, the skin scarred purple.

I begin to wash her. She raises her feet for me in turn. I knead and massage the lax toes through the soft milky soap. Soon my eyes close, my head droops. It is rapture, of a kind.

When I have washed her feet I begin to wash her legs. For

this she has to stand in the basin and lean on my shoulder. My hands run up and down her legs from ankle to knee, back and forth, squeezing, stroking, moulding. Her legs are short and sturdy, her calves strong. Sometimes my fingers run behind her knees, tracing the tendons, pressing into the hollows between them. Light as feathers they stray up the backs of her thighs.

I help her to the bed and dry her with a warm towel. I begin to pare and clean her toenails; but already waves of sleepiness are running over me. I catch my head drooping, my body falling forward in a stupor. Carefully I put the scissors aside. Then, fully clothed, I lay myself down head to foot beside her. I fold her legs together in my arms, cradle my head on them, and in an instant am asleep.

I wake up in the dark. The lamp is out, there is a smell of burnt wick. I get up and open the curtains. The girl lies huddled asleep, her knees drawn up to her chest. When I touch her she groans and huddles tighter. 'You are getting cold,' I say, but she hears nothing. I spread a blanket over her, and a second blanket.

First comes the ritual of the washing, for which she is now naked. I wash her feet, as before, her legs, her buttocks. My soapy hand travels between her thighs, incuriously, I find. She raises her arms while I wash her armpits. I wash her belly, her breasts. I push her hair aside and wash her neck, her throat. She is patient. I rinse and dry her.

She lies on the bed and I rub her body with almond oil. I close my eyes and lose myself in the rhythm of the rubbing, while the fire, piled high, roars in the grate.

I feel no desire to enter this stocky little body glistening by now in the firelight. It is a week since words have passed between us. I feed her, shelter her, use her body, if that is what I am doing, in this foreign way. There used to be moments when she stiffened at certain intimacies; but now her body yields when I nuzzle my face into her belly or clasp her feet between my thighs. She yields to everything. Sometimes she slips off into sleep before I am finished. She sleeps as intensely as a child.

As for me, under her blind gaze, in the close warmth of the room, I can undress without embarrassment, baring my thin shanks, my slack genitals, my paunch, my flabby old man's breasts, the turkey-skin of my throat. I find myself moving about unthinkingly in this nakedness, sometimes staying to bask in the fire after the girl has gone to sleep, or sitting in a chair reading.

But more often in the very act of caressing her I am overcome with sleep as if poleaxed, fall into oblivion sprawled upon her body, and wake an hour or two later dizzy, confused, thirsty. These dreamless spells are like death to me, or enchantment, blank, outside time.

One evening, rubbing her scalp with oil, massaging her temples and forehead, I notice in the corner of one eye a greyish puckering as though a caterpillar lay there with its head under her eyelid, grazing.

'What is this?' I ask, tracing the caterpillar with my fingernail.

'That is where they touched me,' she says, and pushed my hand away.

'Does it hurt?'

She shakes her head.

'Let me look.'

It has been growing more and more clear to me that until the marks on this girl's body are deciphered and understood I cannot let go of her. Between thumb and forefinger I part her eyelids. The caterpillar comes to an end, decapitated, at the pink inner rim of the eyelid. There is no other mark. The eye is whole.

I look into the eye. Am I to believe that gazing back at me she sees nothing – my feet perhaps, parts of the room, a hazy circle of light, but at the centre, where I am, only a blur, a blank? I pass my hand slowly in front of her face, watching her pupils. I cannot discern any movement. She does not blink. But she smiles: 'Why do you do that? Do you think I cannot see?' Brown eyes, so brown as to be black.

I touch my lips to her forehead. 'What did they do to you?' I murmur. My tongue is slow, I sway on my feet with exhaustion. 'Why don't you want to tell me?'

She shakes her head. On the edge of oblivion it comes back to me that my fingers, running over her buttocks, have felt a phantom criss-cross of ridges under the skin. 'Nothing is worse than what we can imagine,' I mumble. She gives no sign that she has even heard me. I slump on the couch, drawing her down beside me, yawning. 'Tell me,' I want to say, 'don't make a mystery of it, pain is only pain'; but words elude me. My arm folds around her, my lips are at the hollow of her ear, I struggle to speak; then blackness falls.

I have relieved her of the shame of begging and installed her in the barracks kitchen as a scullery-maid. 'From the kitchen to the Magistrate's bed in sixteen easy steps' – that is how the soldiers talk of the kitchenmaids. Another of their sayings: 'What is the last thing the Magistrate does when he leaves in the morning? – He shuts his latest girl in the oven.' The smaller a town the more richly it hums with gossip. There are no private affairs here. Gossip is the air we breathe.

For part of the day she washes dishes, peels vegetables, helps to bake bread and prepare the humdrum round of porridge, soup and stew that the soldiers are fed. There are, besides her, the old lady who has ruled over the kitchen almost as long as I have been magistrate, and two girls, the younger of whom ascended the sixteen stairs once or twice last year. At first I am afraid these two will band together against her; but no, they seem quickly to make friends. Passing the kitchen door on my way out I hear, muffled by the steamy warmth, voices, soft chatter, giggles. I am amused to detect in myself the faintest stab of jealousy.

'Do you mind the work?' I ask her.

'I like the other girls. They are nice.'

'At least it's better than begging, isn't it?'

'Yes.'

34

The three girls sleep together in a small room a few doors from the kitchen, if they do not happen to be sleeping elsewhere. It is to this room that she finds her way in the dark if I send her away in the night or the early morning. No doubt her friends have prattled about these trysts of hers, and the details are all over the marketplace. The older a man the more grotesque people find his couplings, like the spasms of a dying animal. I cannot play the part of a man of iron or a saintly widower. Sniggers, jokes, knowing looks – these are part of the price I am resigned to paying.

'Do you like it, living in a town?' I ask her cautiously.

'I like it most of the time. There is more to do.'

'Are there things you miss?'

'I miss my sister.'

'If you really want to go back,' I say, 'I will have you taken.'

'Taken where?' she says. She lies on her back with her hands placidly over her breasts. I lie beside her, speaking softly. This is where the break always falls. This is where my hand, caressing her belly, seems as awkward as a lobster. The erotic impulse, if that is what it has been, withers; with surprise I see myself clutched to this stolid girl, unable to remember what I ever desired in her, angry with myself for wanting and not wanting her.

She herself is oblivious of my swings of mood. Her days have begun to settle into a routine with which she seems content. In the morning after I have left she comes to sweep and dust the apartment. Then she helps in the kitchen with the midday meal. Her afternoons are mainly her own. After the evening meal, after all the pots and pans have been scoured, the floor washed, the fire damped, she leaves her fellows and picks her way up the stairs to me. She undresses and lies down, waiting for my inexplicable attentions. Perhaps I sit beside her stroking her body, waiting for a flush of blood that never truly comes. Perhaps I simply blow out the lamp and settle down with her. In the dark she soon forgets me and falls asleep. So I lie beside this healthy young body while it knits itself in sleep into ever

35

sturdier health, working in silence even at the points of irremediable damage, the eyes, the feet, to be whole again.

I cast my mind back, trying to recover an image of her as she was before. I must believe that I saw her on the day she was brought in by the soldiers roped neck to neck with the other barbarian prisoners. I know that my gaze must have passed over her when, together with the others, she sat in the barracks yard waiting for whatever was to happen next. My eye passed over her; but I have no memory of that passage. On that day she was still unmarked; but I must believe she was unmarked as I must believe she was once a child, a little girl in pigtails running after her pet lamb in a universe where somewhere far away I strode in the pride of my life. Strain as I will, my first image remains of the kneeling beggar-girl.

I have not entered her. From the beginning my desire has not taken on that direction, that directedness. Lodging my dry old man's member in that blood-hot sheath makes me think of acid in milk, ashes in honey, chalk in bread. When I look at her naked body and my own, I find it impossible to believe that once upon a time I imagined the human form as a flower radiating out from a kernel in the loins. These bodies of hers and mine are diffuse, gaseous, centreless, at one moment spinning about a vortex here, at another curdling, thickening elsewhere; but often also flat, blank. I know what to do with her no more than one cloud in the sky knows what to do with another.

I watch her as she undresses, hoping to capture in her movements a hint of an old free state. But even the motion with which she pulls the smock up over her head and throws it aside is crabbed, defensive, trammelled, as though she were afraid of striking unseen obstacles. Her face has the look of something that knows itself watched.

From a trapper I have bought a little silver-fox cub. It is no more than a few months old, barely weaned, with teeth like a fine saw-edge. The first day she took it with her to the kitchen, but it was terrified by the fire and the noise, so now I keep it upstairs, where it cowers all day under the furniture. During the night I sometimes hear the click-click of its claws on the wooden floors as it roams about. It laps from a saucer of milk and eats scraps of cooked meat. It cannot be housetrained; the rooms have begun to smell of its droppings; but it is still too early to let it run loose in the yard. Every few days I call in the cook's grandson to crawl behind the cabinet and under the chairs to clean up the mess.

'It's a very pretty little creature,' I say.

She shrugs. 'Animals belong outdoors.'

'Do you want me to take it to the lake and let it go?'

'You can't do that, it is too young, it would starve to death or dogs would catch it.'

So the fox cub stays. Sometimes I see its sharp snout peeking out from a dark corner. Otherwise it is only a noise in the night and a pervasive tang of urine as I wait for it to grow big enough to be disposed of.

'People will say I keep two wild animals in my rooms, a fox and a girl.'

She does not see the joke, or does not like it. Her lips close, her gaze settles rigidly on the wall, I know she is doing her best to glare at me. My heart goes out to her, but what can I do? Whether I appear to her decked in my robes of office or whether I stand naked before her or whether I tear open my breast for her, I am the same man. 'I am sorry,' I say, the words falling inertly from my mouth. I reach out five dough-fingers and stroke her hair. 'Of course it is not the same.'

One after another I interview those men who were on duty while the prisoners were being questioned. From each I get the same account: they hardly spoke to the prisoners, they were not permitted to enter the room where the interrogations took place, they cannot tell me what went on in there. But from the sweeping-woman I get a description of the room itself: 'Just a little table, and stools, three stools, and a mat in the corner, otherwise quite bare . . . No, no fire, only a brazier. I used to empty out the ashes.'

Now that life has returned to normal the room is in use again. At my request the four soldiers who are quartered there drag their chests out on to the gallery, pile their sleeping-mats, plates and mugs on top of them, take down their strings of laundry. I close the door and stand in the empty room. The air is still and cold. Already the lake is beginning to freeze over. The first snows have fallen. Far away I hear the bells of a pony-cart. I close my eyes and make an effort to imagine the room as it must have been two months ago during the Colonel's visit; but it is difficult to lose myself in reverie with the four young men dawdling outside, chafing their hands together, stamping their feet, murmuring, impatient for me to go, their warm breath forming puffs in the air.

I kneel down to examine the floor. It is clean, it is swept daily, it is like the floor of any room. Above the fireplace on the wall and ceiling there is soot. There is also a mark the size of my hand where soot has been rubbed into the wall. Otherwise the walls are blank. What signs can I be looking for? I open the door and motion to the men to bring their belongings back.

A second time I interview the two guards who were on duty in the yard. 'Tell me exactly what happened when prisoners were questioned. Tell me what you yourselves saw.'

The taller one replies, a boy with a long jaw and an eager air whom I have always liked. 'The officer . . .'

'The police officer?'

'Yes . . . The police officer would come to the hall where the prisoners were kept and he would point. We would fetch the prisoners he wanted and take them out to be questioned. Afterwards we would take them back.'

'One at a time?'

'Not always. Sometimes two.'

'You know that one of the prisoners afterwards died. Do you remember that prisoner? Do you know what they did to him?'

'We heard he went berserk and attacked them.'

'Yes?'

'That is what we heard. I helped to carry him back to the

hall. Where they all slept. He was breathing strangely, very deep and fast. That was the last I saw of him. He was dead the next day.'

'Go on. I am listening. I want you to tell me everything you can remember.'

The boy's face is strained. I am sure he has been advised not to talk. 'That man was questioned longer than anyone else. I saw him sitting by himself in a corner, after he had been in the first time, holding his head.' His eyes flicker towards his companion. 'He would not eat anything. He was not hungry. His daughter was with him: she tried to make him take food but he would not.'

'What happened to his daughter?'

'She was also questioned, but not so long.'

'Go on.'

But he has nothing more to tell me.

'Listen,' I say: 'we both know who the daughter is. She is the girl who stays with me. It is not a secret. Now go on: tell me what happened.'

'I do not know, sir! Most of the time I was not there.' He appeals to his friend, but his friend is mute. 'Sometimes there was screaming, I think they beat her, but I was not there. When I came off duty I would go away.'

'You know that today she cannot walk. They broke her feet. Did they do these things to her in front of the other man, her father?'

'Yes, I think so.'

'And you know that she cannot see properly any more. When did they do that?'

'Sir, there were many prisoners to take care of, some of them sick! I knew that her feet were broken but I knew nothing about her being blind till long afterwards. There was nothing I could do, I did not want to become involved in a matter I did not understand!'

His friend has nothing to add. I dismiss them. 'Do not be afraid because you have spoken to me,' I say.

In the night the dream comes back. I am trudging across the

snow of an endless plain towards a group of tiny figures playing around a snowcastle. As I approach the children sidle away or melt into the air. Only one figure remains, a hooded child sitting with its back to me. I circle around the child, who continues to pat snow on the sides of the castle, till I can peer under the hood. The face I see is blank, featureless; it is the face of an embryo or a tiny whale; it is not a face at all but another part of the human body that bulges under the skin; it is white; it is the snow itself. Between numb fingers I hold out a coin.

Winter has settled in. The wind blows from the north, and will blow incessantly for the next four months. Standing at the window with my forehead against the cold glass I hear it whistle in the eaves, lifting and dropping a loose roof-tile. Flurries of dust chase across the square, dust patters against the pane. The sky is full of fine dust, the sun swims up into an orange sky and sets copper-red. Now and again there are squalls of snow which briefly fleck the earth with white. The siege of winter is on. The fields are empty, no one has reason to go outside the town walls except those few who make a livelihood by hunting. The twice-weekly parade of the garrison has been suspended, the soldiers have permission to quit the barracks if they wish and live in the town, for there is little for them to do but drink and sleep. When I walk the ramparts in the early morning half the watchposts are empty and the numbed sentries on duty, swathed in furs, struggle to raise a hand in salute. They might as well be in their beds. For the duration of the winter the Empire is safe: beyond the eye's reach the barbarians too, huddled about their stoves, are gritting their teeth against the cold.

There have been no barbarian visitors this year. It used to be that groups of nomads would visit the settlement in winter to pitch their tents outside the walls and engage in barter, exchanging wool, skins, felts and leatherwork for cotton goods, tea, sugar, beans, flour. We prize barbarian leatherwork, particularly the sturdy boots they sew. In the past I have encouraged commerce but forbidden payment in money. I have also tried to keep the taverns closed to them. Above all I do not want to see a parasite settlement grow up on the fringes of the town populated with beggars and vagrants enslaved to strong drink. It always pained me in the old days to see these people fall victim to the guile of shopkeepers, exchanging their goods for trinkets, lying drunk in the gutter, and confirming thereby the settlers' litany of prejudice: that barbarians are lazy, immoral, filthy, stupid. Where civilization entailed the corruption of barbarian virtues and the creation of a dependent people, I decided, I was opposed to civilization; and upon this resolution I based the conduct of my administration. (I say this who now keep a barbarian girl for my bed!)

But this year a curtain has fallen all along the frontier. From our ramparts we stare out over the wastes. For all we know, keener eyes than ours stare back. Commerce is at an end. Since the news arrived from the capital that whatever might be necessary to safeguard the Empire would be done, regardless of cost, we have returned to an age of raids and armed vigilance. There is nothing to do but keep our swords bright, watch and wait.

I spend my time in my old recreations. I read the classics; I continue to catalogue my various collections; I collate what maps we have of the southern desert region; on days when the wind does not bite so keenly I take out a party of diggers to clear drift-sand from the excavations; and once or twice a week I set off by myself in the early morning to hunt antelope along the lakeshore.

A generation ago there were antelope and hares in such numbers that watchmen with dogs had to patrol the fields by night to protect the young wheat. But under pressure from the settlement, particularly from dogs running wild and hunting in packs, the antelope have retreated eastward and northward to the lower reaches of the river and the far shore. Now the hunter must be prepared to ride at least an hour before he can begin his stalk.

Sometimes, on a good morning, I am enabled to live again all the strength and swiftness of my manhood. Like a wraith I glide from brake to brake. Shod in boots that have soaked in thirty years of grease, I wade through icy water. Over my coat I wear my huge old bearskin. Rime forms on my beard but my fingers are warm in their mittens. My eyes are sharp, my hearing is keen, I sniff the air like a hound, I feel a pure exhilaration.

Today I leave my horse hobbled where the line of marshgrass ends on the bleak south-west shore and begin to push my way through the reeds. The wind blows chill and dry straight into my eyes, the sun is suspended like an orange on an horizon streaked black and purple. Almost at once, with absurd good fortune, I come upon a waterbuck, a ram with heavy curved horns, shaggy in his winter coat, standing sideways on to me, teetering as he stretches up for the reed-tips. From not thirty paces I see the placid circular motion of his jaw, hear the splash of his hooves. Around his fetlocks I can make out circlets of ice-drops.

I am barely attuned yet to my surroundings; still, as the ram lifts himself, folding his forelegs under his chest, I slide the gun up and sight behind his shoulder. The movement is smooth and steady, but perhaps the sun glints on the barrel, for in his descent he turns his head and sees me. His hooves touch ice with a click, his jaw stops in mid-motion, we gaze at each other.

My pulse does not quicken: evidently it is not important to me that the ram die.

He chews again, a single scythe of the jaws, and stops. In the clear silence of the morning I find an obscure sentiment lurking at the edge of my consciousness. With the buck before me suspended in immobility, there seems to be time for all things, time even to turn my gaze inward and see what it is that has robbed the hunt of its savour: the sense that this has become no longer a morning's hunting but an occasion on which either the proud ram bleeds to death on the ice or the old hunter misses his aim; that for the duration of this frozen moment the stars are locked in a configuration in which events are not themselves but stand for other things. Behind my paltry cover I stand trying to shrug off this irritating and uncanny feeling, till the buck wheels and with a whisk of his tail and a brief splash of hooves disappears into the tall reeds.

I trudge on purposelessly for an hour before I turn back.

'Never before have I had the feeling of not living my own life on my own terms,' I tell the girl, struggling to explain what happened. She is unsettled by talk like this, by the demand I seem to be making on her to respond. 'I do not see,' she says. She shakes her head. 'Didn't you want to shoot this buck?'

For a long while there is silence between us.

'If you want to do something, you do it,' she says very firmly. She is making an effort to be clear; but perhaps she intends, 'If you had wanted to do it you would have done it.' In the makeshift language we share there are no nuances. She has a fondness for facts, I note, for pragmatic dicta; she dislikes fancy, questions, speculations; we are an ill-matched couple. Perhaps that is how barbarian children are brought up: to live by rote, by the wisdom of the fathers as handed down.

'And you,' I say. 'Do you do whatever you want?' I have a sense of letting go, of being carried dangerously far by the words. 'Are you here in bed with me because it is what you want?'

She lies naked, her oiled skin glowing a vegetal gold in the firelight. There are moments – I feel the onset of one now – when the desire I feel for her, usually so obscure, flickers into a shape I can recognize. My hand stirs, strokes her, fits itself to the contour of her breast.

She does not answer my words, but I plunge on, embracing her tightly, speaking thick and muffled into her ear: 'Come, tell me why you are here.'

'Because there is nowhere else to go.'

'And why do I want you here?'

She wriggles in my grasp, clenches her hand into a fist between her chest and mine. 'You want to talk all the time,' she complains. The simplicity of the moment is over; we sepa-

43

rate and lie silent side by side. What bird has the heart to sing in a thicket of thorns? 'You should not go hunting if you do not enjoy it.'

I shake my head. That is not the meaning of the story, but what is the use of arguing? I am like an incompetent school-master, fishing about with my maieutic forceps when I ought to be filling her with the truth.

She speaks. 'You are always asking me that question, so I will now tell you. It was a fork, a kind of fork with only two teeth. There were little knobs on the teeth to make them blunt. They put it in the coals till it was hot, then they touched you with it, to burn you. I saw the marks where they had burned people.'

Is this the question I asked? I want to protest but instead listen on, chilled.

'They did not burn me. They said they would burn my eyes out, but they did not. The man brought it very close to my face and made me look at it. They held my eyelids open. But I had nothing to tell them. That was all.

'That was when the damage came. After that I could not see properly any more. There was a blur in the middle of everything I looked at; I could see only around the edges. It is difficult to explain.

'But now it is getting better. The left eye is getting better. That is all.'

I take her face between my hands and stare into the dead centres of her eyes, from which twin reflections of myself stare solemnly back. 'And this?' I say, touching the worm-like scar in the corner.

'That is nothing. That is where the iron touched me. It made a little burn. It is not sore.' She pushes my hands away.

'What do you feel towards the men who did this?'

She lies thinking a long time. Then she says, 'I am tired of talking.'

There are other times when I suffer fits of resentment against my bondage to the ritual of the oiling and rubbing, the drowsiness, the slump into oblivion. I cease to comprehend what pleasure I can ever have found in her obstinate, phlegmatic body, and even discover in myself stirrings of outrage. I become withdrawn, irritable; the girl turns her back and goes to sleep.

In this moody state I pay a visit one evening to the rooms on the second floor of the inn. As I climb the rickety outside stairway a man I do not recognize hurries down past me, ducking his head. I knock at the second door along the corridor and enter. The room is just as I remember it: the bed neatly made, the shelf above it packed with trinkets and toys, two candles burning, a glow of warmth coming from the great flue that runs along the wall, an odour of orange-blossom in the air. The girl herself is occupied in front of the mirror. She gives a start at my entry, but rises smiling to welcome me and bolts the door. Nothing seems more natural than to seat her on the bed and begin to undress her. With little shrugs she helps me bare her trim body. 'How I have missed you!' she sighs. 'What a pleasure to be back!' I whisper. And what a pleasure to be lied to so flatteringly! I embrace her, bury myself in her, lose myself in her soft bird-like flurries. The body of the other one, closed, ponderous, sleeping in my bed in a faraway room, seems beyond comprehension. Occupied in these suave pleasures, I cannot imagine what ever drew me to that alien body. The girl in my arms flutters, pants, cries as she comes to a climax. Smiling with joy, sliding into a languorous half-sleep, it occurs to me that I cannot even recall the other one's face. 'She is incomplete!' I say to myself. Though the thought begins to float away at once, I cling to it. I have a vision of her closed eyes and closed face filming over with skin. Blank, like a fist beneath a black wig, the face grows out of the throat and out of the blank body beneath it, without aperture, without entry. I shudder with revulsion in the arms of my little bird-woman, hug her to me.

When later in the middle of the night I ease myself out of her arms, she whimpers but does not awaken. I dress in the dark, close the door behind me, grope my way down the stairs, hurry back home with snow crunching underfoot and an icy wind boring into my back.

I light a candle and bend over the form to which, it seems, I am in a measure enslaved. Lightly I trace the lines of her face with my fingertip: the clear jaw, the high cheekbones, the wide mouth. Lightly I touch her eyelids. I am sure she is awake, though she gives no sign.

I shut my eyes, breathe deeply to still my agitation, and concentrate wholly on seeing her through my blind fingertips. Is she pretty? The girl I have just left, the girl she may perhaps (I suddenly realize) smell on me, is very pretty, there is no question about that: the acuteness of my pleasure in her is sharpened by the elegance of her tiny body, its manners, its movements. But of this one there is nothing I can say with certainty. There is no link I can define between her womanhood and my desire. I cannot even say for sure that I desire her. All this erotic behaviour of mine is indirect: I prowl about her, touching her face, caressing her body, without entering her or finding the urge to do so. I have just come from the bed of a woman for whom, in the year I have known her, I have not for a moment had to interrogate my desire: to desire her has meant to enfold her and enter her, to pierce her surface and stir the quiet of her interior into an ecstatic storm; then to retreat, to subside, to wait for desire to reconstitute itself. But with this woman it is as if there is no interior, only a surface across which I hunt back and forth seeking entry. Is this how her torturers felt hunting their secret, whatever they thought it was? For the first time I feel a dry pity for them: how natural a mistake to believe that you can burn or tear or hack your way into the secret body of the other! The girl lies in my bed, but there is no good reason why it should be a bed. I behave in some ways like a lover – I undress her, I bathe her, I stroke her, I sleep beside her – but I might equally well tie her to a chair and beat her, it would be no less intimate.

It is not that something is in the course of happening to me that happens to some men of a certain age, a downward progress from libertinage to vengeful actions of impotent yearning. If a change in my moral being were occurring I would feel it; nor would I have undertaken this evening's reassuring experiment. I am the same man I always was; but time has broken, something has fallen in upon me from the sky, at random, from nowhere: this body in my bed, for which I am responsible, or so it seems, otherwise why do I keep it? For the time being, perhaps forever, I am simply bewildered. It seems all one whether I lie down beside her and fall asleep or fold her in a sheet and bury her in the snow. Nevertheless, bending over her, touching my finger-tips to her forehead, I am careful not to spill the wax.

Whether she guesses where I have been I cannot decide; but the next night, when I am lulled almost to sleep by the rhythm of the oiling and rubbing, I feel my hand stopped, held, guided down between her legs. For a while it rests against her sex; then I shake more of the warm oil on to my fingers and begin to caress her. Quickly the tension gathers in her body; she arches and shudders and pushes my hand away. I continue to rub her body till I too relax and am overtaken with sleep.

I experience no excitement during this the most collaborative act we have yet undertaken. It brings me no closer to her and seems to affect her as little. I search her face the next morning: it is blank. She dresses and stumbles down to her day in the kitchen.

I am disquieted. 'What do I have to do to move you?': these are the words I hear in my head in the subterranean murmur that has begun to take the place of conversation. 'Does no one move you?'; and with a shift of horror I behold the answer that has been waiting all the time offer itself to me in the image of a face masked by two black glassy insect eyes from which there comes no reciprocal gaze but only my doubled image cast back at me.

I shake my head in a fury of disbelief. *No! No! No!* I cry to myself. It is I who am seducing myself, out of vanity, into these meanings and correspondences. What depravity is it that is creeping upon me? I search for secrets and answers, no matter how bizarre, like an old woman reading tea-leaves. There is nothing to link me with torturers, people who sit waiting like beetles in dark cellars. How can I believe that a bed is anything but a bed, a woman's body anything but a site of joy? I must assert my distance from Colonel Joll! I will not suffer for his crimes!

I begin to visit the girl at the inn regularly. There are moments during the day, in my office behind the courtroom, when my attention wanders and I drift into erotic reverie, grow hot and swollen with excitement, linger over her body like a moony lustful youth; then reluctantly I have to recall myself to the tedium of paperwork or walk over to the window and stare into the street. I remember how in the first years of my appointment here I used to roam the obscurer quarters of the town toward dusk, shadowing my face in my cloak; how sometimes a restless wife, leaning over the half-door with the hearthfire gleaming behind her, would answer my gaze without flinching; how I would fall into conversation with young girls promenading in twos and threes, buy them sherbet, then perhaps lead one away into the darkness to the old granary and a bed of sacks. If there was anything to be envied in a posting to the frontier, my friends told me, it was the easy morals of the oases, the long scented summer evenings, the complaisant sloe-eyed women. For years I wore the well-fed look of a prize boar. Later that promiscuity modulated into more discreet relations with housekeepers and girls lodged sometimes upstairs in my rooms but more often downstairs with the kitchen help, and into liaisons with girls at the inn. I found that I needed women less frequently; I spent more time on my work, my hobbies, my antiquarianism, my cartography.

Not only that; there were unsettling occasions when in the middle of the sexual act I felt myself losing my way like a storyteller losing the thread of his story. I thought with a shiver of those figures of fun, fat old men whose overburdened hearts stop beating, who pass away in the arms of their loves with an apology on their lips and have to be carried out and dumped in a dark alley to save the reputation of the house. The climax to the act itself became remote, puny, an oddity. Sometimes I drifted to a halt, sometimes went mechanically through to the end. For weeks and months I would retire into celibacy. The old delight in the warmth and shapeliness of women's bodies did not desert me, but there was a new puzzlement. Did I really want to enter and claim possession of these beautiful creatures? Desire seemed to bring with it a pathos of distance and separation which it was futile to deny. Nor could I always see why one part of my body, with its unreasonable cravings and false promises, should be heeded over any other as a channel of desire. Sometimes my sex seemed to me another being entirely, a stupid animal living parasitically upon me, swelling and dwindling according to autonomous appetites, anchored to my flesh with claws I could not detach. Why do I have to carry you about from woman to woman, I asked: simply because you were born without legs? Would it make any difference to you if you were rooted in a cat or a dog instead of in me?

Yet at other times, and particularly in the last year, with the girl whose nickname at the inn is The Star but whom I have always thought of as a bird, I felt again the power of the old sensual enchantment, swam out into her body and was transported to the old limits of pleasure. So I thought: 'It is nothing but a matter of age, of cycles of desire and apathy in a body that is slowly cooling and dying. When I was young the mere smell of a woman would arouse me; now it is evidently only the sweetest, the youngest, the newest who have that power. One of these days it will be little boys.' With some distaste I looked forward to my last years in this bountiful oasis.

Three nights in succession, now, I visit her in her little room, bringing presents of cananga oil, sweets, and a jar of the smoked fish-roe I know she loves to wolf down in private. When I embrace her she closes her eyes; tremors of what seem to be delight run through her. The friend who first recommended her to me spoke of her talents: 'It is all playacting of course,' he said, 'but in her case the difference is that she believes in the role she plays.' For myself, I find I do not care. Captivated by her performance, I open my eyes in the midst of all the fluttering and shivering and moaning, then sink back into the dark river of my own pleasure.

I spend three days of sensual languor, heavy-lidded, sleekly aroused, daydreaming. I return to my rooms after midnight and slip into bed, paying no attention to the obdurate form beside me. If I am woken in the morning by the sound of her preparations, I feign sleep till she is gone.

Once, happening to pass the open kitchen door, I glance in. Through wraiths of steam I see a stocky girl seated at a table preparing food. 'I know who that is,' I think to myself with surprise; nevertheless, the image that persists in my memory as I cross the yard is of the pile of green marrows on the table in front of her. Deliberately I try to shift my mind's gaze from the marrows back to the hands that slice them, and from the hands to the face. I detect in myself a reluctance, a resistance. My regard remains dazedly fixed on the marrows, on the gleam of light on their wet skins. As if with a will of its own, it does not move. So I begin to face the truth of what I am trying to do: to obliterate the girl. I realize that if I took a pencil to sketch her face I would not know where to start. Is she truly so featureless? With an effort I concentrate my mind on her. I see a figure in a cap and heavy shapeless coat standing unsteadily, bent forward, straddle-legged, supporting itself on sticks. How ugly, I say to myself. My mouth forms the ugly word. I am surprised by it but I do not resist: she is ugly, ugly.

I come back on the fourth night in a bad temper, thrashing about my rooms noisily, not caring who is woken. The evening has been a failure, the current of renewed desire is broken. I throw my boots on the floor and climb into bed spoiling for a quarrel, longing for someone to blame, ashamed too of my childishness. What this woman beside me is doing in my life I cannot comprehend. The thought of the strange ecstasies I have approached through the medium of her incomplete body fills me with a dry revulsion, as if I had spent nights copulating with a dummy of straw and leather. What could I ever have seen in her? I try to recall her as she was before the doctors of pain began their ministrations. It is impossible that my gaze did not pass over her as she sat with the other barbarian prisoners in the yard the day they were brought in. Somewhere in the honeycomb of my brain, I am convinced, the memory is lodged; but I am unable to bring it back. I can remember the woman with the baby, even the baby itself. I can remember every detail: the frayed edge of the woollen shawl, the patina of sweat under the wisps of fine baby-hair. I can remember the bony hands of the man who died; I believe I can even, with an effort, recompose his face. But beside him, where the girl should be, there is a space, a blankness.

I wake up in the night with the girl shaking me and the echo of a thin moan still hanging in the air. 'You were shouting in your sleep,' she says. 'You woke me up.'

'What was I shouting?'

She mumbles something, turns her back on me.

Later in the night she wakes me again: 'You were shouting.'

Thick-headed and confused, angry too, I try to look into myself but see only a vortex and at the heart of the vortex oblivion.

'Is it a dream?' she says.

'I cannot remember any dream.'

Can it be that the dream of the hooded child building the snowcastle has been coming back? If it has, surely the taste or the smell or the afterglow of the dream would linger with me.

'There is something I must ask you,' I say. 'Do you remember when you were brought here, into the barracks yard, for the first time? The guards made you all sit down. Where did you sit? Which way did you face?'

Through the window I can see streaks of cloud racing across the face of the moon. Out of the darkness beside me she speaks: 'They made us sit together in the shade. I was next to my father.'

I summon up the image of her father. In silence I try to re-create the heat, the dust, the smell of all those tired bodies. In the shade of the barracks wall I seat the prisoners one by one, all that I can remember. I put together the woman with the baby, her woollen shawl, her bare breast. The baby wails, I hear the wail, it is too tired to drink. The mother, bedraggled, thirsty, looks at me, wondering if I can be appealed to. Next come two hazy forms. Hazy but present: I know that with an effort half of memory, half of imagination, I can fill them out. Then comes the girl's father, his bony hands folded before him. His cap is tipped over his eyes, he does not look up. Now I turn to the space beside him.

'On which side of your father were you sitting?'

'I sat to his right.'

The space to the right of the man remains blank. Concentrating painfully I see even the individual pebbles on the earth beside him and the texture of the wall behind.

'Tell me what you were doing.'

'Nothing. We were all very tired. We had walked since before dawn. We stopped to rest only once. We were tired and thirsty.'

'Did you see me?'

'Yes, we all saw you.'

I clasp my arms around my knees and concentrate. The space beside the man remains empty, but a faint sense of the presence of the girl, an aura, begins to emerge. *Now!* I urge myself: now I will open my eyes and she will be there! I open my eyes. In the dim light I make out her shape beside me. With a rush of feeling I stretch out to touch her hair, her face. There is no answering life. It is like caressing an urn or a ball, something which is all surface.

'I have been trying to remember you as you were before all this happened,' I say. 'I find it difficult. It is a pity you can't tell me.' I do not expect a denial, and it does not come.

A detachment of new conscripts has arrived to take the places of men who have completed their three-year spell on the frontier and are ready to leave for their homes. The detachment is led by a young officer who is to join the staff here.

I invite him, with two of his colleagues, to dine with me at the inn. The evening goes well: the food is good, the drink plentiful, my guest has stories to tell about his journey, undertaken in a hard season in a region wholly foreign to him. He lost three men on the way, he says: one left his tent in the night to answer a call of nature and never returned; two more deserted almost within sight of the oasis, slipping away to hide in the reeds. Troublemakers, he calls them, whom he was not sorry to be rid of. Still, do I not think their desertion was foolish? Very foolish, I reply; has he any idea why they deserted? No, he says: they were fairly treated, everyone was fairly treated; but then of course conscripts . . . He shrugs. They would have done better to desert earlier, I suggest. The country around here is inhospitable. They are dead men if they have not found shelter by now.

We speak of the barbarians. He is convinced, he says, that for part of the way he was trailed at a distance by barbarians. Are you sure they were barbarians? I ask. Who else could they have been? he replies. His colleagues concur.

I like this young man's energy, his interest in the new sights of the frontier region. His achievement in bringing his men through in this dead season is commendable. When our companions plead the lateness of the hour and depart, I press him to stay. Past midnight we sit talking and drinking. I hear the latest news from the capital, which I have not seen for so long. I tell him of some of the places I look back on with nostalgia: the pavilion gardens where musicians perform for the strolling crowds and one's feet rustle through fallen autumn chestnut leaves; a bridge I remember from which one sees the reflection of the moon on the water that ripples around the pediments in the shape of a flower of paradise.

'The rumour going about brigade headquarters,' he says, 'is that there will be a general offensive against the barbarians in the spring to push them back from the frontier into the mountains.'

I am sorry to break off the train of reminiscing. I do not want to end the evening with a wrangle. Nevertheless I respond. 'I am sure it is only a rumour: they cannot seriously intend to do that. The people we call barbarians are nomads, they migrate between the lowlands and the uplands every year, that is their way of life. They will never permit themselves to be bottled up in the mountains.'

He looks at me oddly. For the first time this evening I feel a barrier descend, the barrier between the military and the civilian. 'But surely,' he says, 'if we are to be frank, that is what war is about: compelling a choice on someone who would not otherwise make it.' He surveys me with the arrogant candour of a young graduate of the War College. I am sure that he is remembering the story, which must by now have gone the rounds, of how I withheld my co-operation from an officer of the Bureau. I think I know what he sees before him: a minor civilian administrator sunk, after years in this backwater, in slothful native ways, outmoded in his thinking, ready to gamble the security of the Empire for a makeshift, insecure peace.

He leans forward, wearing an air of deferential boyish puzzlement: I am more and more convinced he is playing with me. 'Tell me, sir, in confidence,' he says, 'what are these barbarians dissatisfied about? What do they want from us?'

I ought to be cautious but I am not. I ought to yawn, evade his question, end the evening; but I find myself rising to the bait. (When will I learn to keep a cunning tongue?)

'They want an end to the spread of settlements across their land. They want their land back, finally. They want to be free to move about with their flocks from pasture to pasture as they used to.' It is not too late to put a stop to the lecture. Instead I hear my voice rise in tone and abandon myself regretfully to the intoxication of anger. 'I will say nothing of the recent raids carried out on them, quite without justification, and followed by acts of wanton cruelty, since the security of the Empire was at stake, or so I am told. It will take years to patch up the damage done in those few days. But let that pass, let me rather tell you what I find disheartening as an administrator, even in times of peace, even when border relations are good. There is a time in the year, you know, when the nomads visit us to trade. Well: go to any stall in the market during that time and see who gets short-weighted and cheated and shouted at and bullied. See who is forced to leave his womenfolk behind in the camp for fear they will be insulted by the soldiers. See who lies drunk in the gutter, and see who kicks him where he lies. It is this contempt for the barbarians, contempt which is shown by the meanest ostler or peasant farmer, that I as magistrate have had to contend with for twenty years. How do you eradicate contempt, especially when that contempt is founded on nothing more substantial than differences in table manners, variations in the structure of the eyelid? Shall I tell you what I sometimes wish? I wish that these barbarians would rise up and teach us a lesson, so that we would learn to respect them. We think of the country here as ours, part of our Empire – our outpost, our settlement, our market centre. But these people, these barbarians don't think of it like that at all. We have been here more than a hundred years, we have reclaimed land from the desert and built irrigation works and planted fields and built solid homes and put a wall around our town, but they still think of us as visitors, transients. There are old folk alive among them who remember their parents telling them about this oasis as it once was: a well-shaded place by the side of the lake with plenty of grazing even in winter. That is how they still talk about it, perhaps how they still *see* it, as though not one spadeful of earth had been turned or one brick laid on top of another. They do not doubt that one of these days we will pack our carts and depart to wherever it was we came from, that our buildings will become homes for mice and lizards, that their beasts will graze on these rich fields we have planted. You smile? Shall I tell you something? Every year the lake-water grows a little more salty. There is a simple explanation – never mind what it is. The barbarians know this fact. At this very moment they are saying to themselves, "Be patient, one of these days their crops will start withering from the salt, they will not be able to feed themselves, they will have to go." That is what they are thinking. That they will outlast us.'

'But we are not going,' the young man says quietly.

'Are you sure?'

'We are not going, therefore they make a mistake. Even if it became necessary to supply the settlement by convoy, we would not go. Because these border settlements are the first line of defence of the Empire. The sooner the barbarians understand that the better.'

Despite his engaging air there is a rigidity to his thought that must derive from his military education. I sigh. I have achieved nothing by letting myself go. His worst suspicion is no doubt confirmed: that I am unsound as well as old-fashioned. And do I really after all believe what I have been saying? Do I really look forward to the triumph of the barbarian way: intellectual torpor, slovenliness, tolerance of disease and death? If we were to disappear would the barbarians spend their afternoons excavating our ruins? Would they preserve our census rolls and our grain-merchants' ledgers in glass cases, or devote themselves to deciphering the script of our love-letters? Is my indignation at the course that Empire takes anything more than the peevishness of an old man who does not want the ease of his last years on the frontier to be disturbed? I try to turn the conversation to more suitable subjects, to horses, hunting, the weather; but it is late, my young friend wants to leave, and I must settle the reckoning for the evening's entertainment.

The children are playing in the snow again. In their midst, with her back to me, is the hooded figure of the girl. At moments, as I struggle towards her, she is obliterated from sight behind the curtain of falling snow. My feet sink so deep that I can barely lift them. Each step takes an age. This is the worst it has snowed in all the dreams.

As I labour towards them the children leave off their play to look at me. They turn their grave shining faces on me, their white breath drifting from them in puffs. I try to smile and touch them as I pass on my way to the girl, but my features are frozen, the smile will not come, there seems to be a sheet of ice covering my mouth. I raise a hand to tear it off: the hand, I find, is thickly gloved, the fingers are frozen inside the glove, when I touch the glove to my face I feel nothing. With ponderous movements I push my way past the children.

Now I begin to see what the girl is doing. She is building a fort of snow, a walled town which I recognize in every detail: the battlements with the four watchtowers, the gate with the porter's hut beside it, the streets and houses, the great square with the barracks compound in one corner. And here is the very spot where I stand! But the square is empty, the whole town is white and mute and empty. I point to the middle of the square. 'You must put people there!' I want to say. No sound comes from my mouth, in which my tongue lies frozen like a fish. Yet she responds. She sits up on her knees and turns her hooded face towards me. I fear, at this last instant, that she will be a disappointment, that the face she will present to me will be obtuse, slick, like an internal organ not meant to live in the light. But no, she is herself, herself as I have never seen her, a smiling child, the light sparkling on her teeth and glancing from her jet-black eyes. 'So this is what it is to see!' I say to myself. I want to speak to her through my clumsy frozen muzzle. 'How do you do all that fine work with your hands in mittens?' I want to say. She smiles kindly on my mumbling. Then she turns back to her fort in the snow.

I emerge from the dream cold and stiff. It is an hour yet to first light, the fire is dead, my scalp feels numb with cold. The girl beside me sleeps huddled in a ball. I get out of bed and with my greatcloak wrapped about me start rebuilding the fire.

The dream has taken root. Night after night I return to the waste of the snowswept square, trudging towards the figure at its centre, reconfirming each time that the town she is building is empty of life.

I ask the girl about her sisters. She has two sisters, the younger, according to her, 'very pretty, but scatterbrained'. 'Would you not like to see your sisters again?' I ask. The blunder hangs grotesquely in the air between us. We both smile. 'Of course,' she says.

I also ask about the period after her imprisonment, when unknown to me she lived in this town under my jurisdiction.

'People were kind to me when they saw I had been left behind. I used to sleep at the inn for a time while my feet were getting better. There was a man who took care of me. He has gone now. He kept horses.' She also mentions the man who gave her the boots she was wearing when I first met her. I ask about other men. 'Yes, there were other men. I did not have a choice. That was how it had to be.'

After this conversation relations with the common soldiers become more strained. Leaving my apartment for the court-house in the morning, I pass one of the rare inspection parades. I am sure that among these men standing to attention with their equipment in bundles at their feet are some who have slept with the girl. It is not that I imagine them sniggering behind their hands. On the contrary, never have I seen them stand more stoically in the frosty wind that whips across the yard. Never has their bearing been more respectful. They would tell me if they could, I know, that we are all men, that any man can lose his head over a woman. Nevertheless, I try to come home later in the evenings to avoid the line of men at the kitchen door.

There is news of the lieutenant's two deserters. A trapper has come upon them frozen to death in a rough shelter not far from the road thirty miles east of here. Though the lieutenant is inclined to leave them there ('Thirty miles there and thirty miles back in this weather: a great deal for men who are no longer men, don't you think?'), I persuade him to send out a party. 'They must have the rites,' I say. 'Besides, it is good for the morale of their comrades. They should not think that they too might die in the desert and lie forgotten. What we can do to ease their dread of having to leave this beautiful earth must be done. After all, it is we who lead them into these dangers.' So the party leaves, and two days later returns with the crooked ice-hard corpses in a cart. I continue to find it strange that men should desert hundreds of miles from home and within a day's march of food and warmth, but I pursue the matter no further. Standing by the graveside in the icebound cemetery while the last rites are performed and the deceased's luckier comrades watch bareheaded, I repeat to myself that by insisting on correct treatment of the bones I am trying to show these young men that death is no annihilation, that we survive as filiations in the memory of those we knew. Yet is it truly for their benefit alone that I mount the ceremony? Am I not also comforting myself? I offer to take over the chore of writing to the parents to inform them of their respective misfortunes. 'It comes more easily to an older man,' I say.

'Wouldn't you like to do something else?' she asks.

Her foot rests in my lap. I am abstracted, lost in the rhythm of rubbing and kneading the swollen ankle. Her question takes me by surprise. It is the first time she has spoken so pointedly. I shrug it off, smile, try to slip back into my trance, not far from sleep and reluctant to be diverted.

The foot stirs in my grip, comes alive, pokes gently into my groin. I open my eyes to the naked golden body on the bed. She lies with her head cradled in her arms, watching me in the indirect way I am by now used to, showing off her firm breasts and her sleek belly, brimming with young animal health. Her toes continue to probe; but in this slack old gentleman kneeling before her in his plum dressing-gown they find no response.

'Another time,' I say, my tongue curling stupidly around the words. As far as I know this is a lie, but I utter it: 'Another time, perhaps.' Then I lift her leg aside and stretch out beside her. 'Old men have no virtue to protect, so what can I say?' It is a lame joke, poorly expressed, and she does not understand it. She slips open my gown and begins to fondle me. After a while I push her hand away.

'You visit other girls,' she whispers. 'You think I do not know?'

I make a peremptory gesture for her to be quiet.

'Do you also treat them like this?' she whispers, and starts to sob.

Though my heart goes out to her, there is nothing I can do. Yet what humiliation for her! She cannot even leave the apartment without tottering and fumbling while she dresses. She is as much a prisoner now as ever before. I pat her hand and sink deeper into gloom.

This is the last night we sleep in the same bed. I move a cot into the parlour and sleep there. Physical intimacy between us ends. 'For the time being,' I say. 'Until the end of winter. It is better so.' She accepts this excuse without a word. When I come home in the evenings she brings me my tea and kneels by the tray to serve me. Then she returns to the kitchen. An hour later she taps her way up the stairs behind the girl with the dinner-tray. We eat together. After the meal I retire to my study or go out for the evening, resuming my neglected social round: chess in the homes of friends, cards with the officers at the inn. I also pay one or two visits upstairs at the inn, but with guilty feelings that spoil the pleasure. Always, when I return, the girl is asleep, and I must tiptoe like an erring husband.

She adapts without complaint to the new pattern. I tell myself that she submits because of her barbarian upbringing. But what do I know of barbarian upbringings? What I call submission may be nothing but indifference. What does it matter to a beggar, a fatherless child, whether I sleep by myself or not as long as she has a roof over her head and food in her belly? I have hitherto liked to think that she cannot fail to see me as a man in the grip of a passion, however perverted and obscure that passion may be, that in the bated silences which make up so much of our intercourse she cannot but feel my gaze pressing in upon her with the weight of a body. I prefer not to dwell on the possibility that what a barbarian upbringing teaches a girl may be not to accommodate a man's every whim, including the whim of neglect, but to see sexual passion, whether in horse or goat or man or woman, as a simple fact of life with the clearest of means and the clearest of ends; so that the confused actions of an aging foreigner who picks her up off the streets and instals her in his apartment so that he can now kiss her feet, now browbeat her, now anoint her with exotic oils, now ignore her, now sleep in her arms all night, now moodily sleep apart, may seem nothing but evidences of impotence, indecisiveness, alienation from his own desires. While I have not ceased to see her as a body maimed, scarred, harmed, she has perhaps by now grown into and become that new deficient body, feeling no more deformed than a cat feels deformed for having claws instead of fingers. I would do well to take these thoughts seriously. More ordinary than I like to think, she may have ways of finding me ordinary too.

III

The air every morning is full of the beating of wings as the birds fly in from the south, circling above the lake before they settle in the salty fingers of the marshes. In the lulls of the wind the cacophony of their hooting, quacking, honking, squawking reaches us like the noise of a rival city on the water: greylag, beangoose, pintail, wigeon, mallard, teal, smew.

The arrival of the first of the migrating waterfowl confirms the earlier signs, the ghost of a new warmth on the wind, the glassy translucence of the lake-ice. Spring is on its way, one of these days it will be time to plant.

Meanwhile it is the season for trapping. Before dawn, parties of men leave for the lake to lay their nets. By mid-morning they are back with huge catches: birds with their necks twisted, slung from poles row upon row by their feet, or crammed alive into wooden cages, screaming with outrage, trampling each other, with sometimes a great silent whooper swan crouched in their midst. Nature's cornucopia: for the next weeks everyone will eat well.

Before I can leave there are two documents to compose. The first is addressed to the provincial governor. 'To repair some of the damage wrought by the forays of the Third Bureau,' I write, 'and to restore some of the goodwill that previously existed, I am undertaking a brief visit to the barbarians.' I sign and seal the letter.

What the second document is to be I do not yet know. A testament? A memoir? A confession? A history of thirty years on the frontier? All that day I sit in a trance at my desk staring at the empty white paper, waiting for words to come. A second day passes in the same way. On the third day I surrender, put the paper back in the drawer, and make preparations to leave. It seems appropriate that a man who does not know what to do with the woman in his bed should not know what to write.

To accompany me I have chosen three men. Two are young conscripts to whose services on secondment I am entitled. The third is an older man born in these parts, a hunter and horse-trader whose wages I will pay out of my own pocket. I call them together the afternoon before we leave. 'I know this is not a good time of year to travel,' I tell them. 'It is a treacherous time, the tail end of winter, spring not yet here. But if we wait longer we will not find the nomads before they start on their migration.' They ask no questions.

To the girl I say simply, 'I am taking you back to your people, or as near as I can, seeing that they are now dispersed.' She gives no sign of rejoicing. I lay at her side the heavy fur I have bought her to travel in, with a rabbitskin cap embroidered in the native fashion, new boots, gloves.

Now that I have committed myself to a course I sleep more easily and even detect within myself something like happiness.

We depart on the third of March, accompanied through the gate and down the road to the lakeside by a ragtag escort of children and dogs. After we pass the irrigation wall and branch off from the river road, taking the track to the right used by no one but hunters and fowlers, our escort begins to dwindle till there are only two stubborn lads trotting behind us, each determined to outlast the other.

The sun has risen but gives off no warmth. The wind beats at us across the lake bringing tears to our eyes. In single file, four men and a woman, four pack-animals, the horses persistently backing to the wind and having to be sawed around, we wind away from the walled town, the bare fields, and eventually from the panting boys.

My plan is to follow this track till we have skirted the lake to the south, then to strike out north-east across the desert towards the valleys of the ranges where the northern nomads winter. It is a route rarely travelled, since the nomads, when they migrate with their flocks, follow the old dead river-bed in a vast sweep east and south. However, it reduces a journey of six weeks to one or two. I have never travelled it myself.

So for the first three days we plod south and then eastward. To our right stretches a plain of wind-eroded clay terraces merging at its extremes into banks of red dust-clouds and then into the yellow hazy sky. To our left is flat marshland, belts of reeds, and the lake on which the central ice-sheet has not melted. The wind blowing over the ice freezes our very breath, so that rather than ride we often walk for long spells in the lee of our horses. The girl winds a scarf around and around her face and, crouching in the saddle, blindly follows her leader.

Two of the pack-horses are loaded with firewood, but this must be conserved for the desert. Once, half buried in driftsand, we come upon a spreading mound-like tamarisk which we hack to pieces for fuel; for the rest we have to be content with bundles of dry reeds. The girl and I sleep side by side in the same tent, huddled in our furs against the cold.

In these early days of the journey we eat well. We have brought salted meat, flour, beans, dried fruit, and there are wildfowl to shoot. But we have to be sparing with water. The marsh-water here in the shallow southern fingers is too salty to be drinkable. One of the men has to wade twenty or thirty paces in, as deep as his calves, to fill the skins, or, better, to break off lumps of ice. Yet even the melted ice-water is so bitter and salty that it can only be drunk with strong red tea. Every year the lake grows more brackish as the river eats into its banks and sweeps salt and alum into the lake. Since the lake has no outflow its mineral content keeps rising, particularly in the south, where tracts of water are seasonally isolated by sand-bars. After the summer flood the fishermen find carp floating belly-up in the shallows. They say that perch are no more to be seen. What will become of the settlement if the lake grows into a dead sea?

After a day of salty tea all of us except the girl begin to suffer from diarrhoea. I am the worst afflicted. I feel keenly the humiliation of the frequent stops, the undressing and dressing with frozen fingers in the lee of a horse while the others wait.

64

I try to drink as little as possible, to the point even that my mind throws up tantalizing images as I ride: a full cask by the wellside with water splashing from the ladle; clean snow. My occasional hunting and hawking, my desultory womanizing, exercises of manhood, have concealed from me how soft my body has grown. After long marches my bones ache, by nightfall I am so tired that I have no appetite. I trudge on till I cannot put one foot in front of the other; then I clamber into the saddle, fold myself in my cloak, and wave one of the men forward to take over the task of picking out the faint track. The wind never lets up. It howls at us across the ice, blowing from nowhere to nowhere, veiling the sky in a cloud of red dust. From the dust there is no hiding: it penetrates our clothing, cakes our skin, sifts into the baggage. We eat with coated tongues, spitting often, our teeth grating. Dust rather than air becomes the medium in which we live. We swim through dust like fish through water.

The girl does not complain. She eats well, she does not get sick, she sleeps soundly all night clenched in a ball in weather so cold I would hug a dog for comfort. She rides all day without a murmur. Once, glancing up, I see that she is riding asleep, her face as peaceful as a baby's.

On the third day the rim of the marshland begins to curve back towards the north and we know that we have rounded the lake. We pitch camp early and spend the last hours of light collecting every scrap of fuel we can while the horses browse for the last time on the meagre marshgrass. Then at dawn on the fourth day we begin the crossing of the ancient lake-bed that stretches another forty miles beyond the marshes.

The terrain is more desolate than anything we have yet seen. Nothing grows on this salty lake-floor, which in places buckles and pushes up in jagged crystalline hexagons a foot wide. There are dangers too: crossing an unusually smooth patch the front horse suddenly plunges through the crust and sinks chest-deep in foul green slime, the man who leads it standing a moment dumbstruck on thin air before he too splashes in. We struggle to haul them out, the salt crust splintering under the hooves of the flailing horse, the hole widening, a brackish stench everywhere. We have not left the lake behind, we now realize: it stretches beneath us here, sometimes under a cover many feet deep, sometimes under a mere parchment of brittle salt. How long since the sun last shone on these dead waters? We light a fire on firmer ground to warm the shivering man and dry his clothes. He shakes his head. 'I always heard, beware of the green patches, but I never saw this happen before,' he says. He is our guide, the one man among us who has travelled east of the lake. After this we push our horses even harder, in a hurry to be off the dead lake, fearful of being lost in a fluid colder than ice, mineral, subterraneous, airless. We bow our heads and drive into the wind, our coats ballooning behind us, picking a way over the jagged salt-shards, avoiding the smooth ground. Through the river of dust that courses majestically across the sky the sun glows like an orange but warms nothing. When darkness falls we batter the tent-pegs into cracks in the rock-hard salt; we burn our firewood at an extravagant rate and like sailors pray for land.

On the fifth day we leave the lake-floor behind and pass through a belt of smooth crystalline salt which soon gives way to sand and stone. Everyone is heartened, even the horses, which during the crossing of the salt have had nothing but a few handfuls of linseed and a bucketful of brackish water. Their condition is visibly deteriorating.

As for the men, they do not grumble. The fresh meat is giving out but there remain the salt meat and dried beans and plenty of flour and tea, the staples of the road. At each halt we brew tea and fry little fatcakes, delicious morsels to the hungry. The men do the cooking: being shy of the girl, unsure of her standing, unsure most of all what we are doing taking her to the barbarians, they barely address her, avoid looking at her, and certainly do not ask for her help with the food. I do not push her forward, hoping that constraint will disappear on the road. I picked these men because they were hardy and honest and willing. They follow me as lightheartedly as they can under these conditions, though by now the brave lacquered armour the two young soldiers wore when we passed through the great gate is strapped in bundles on the pack-horses and their scabbards are full of sand.

The sand-flats begin to modulate into duneland. Our progress slows as we toil up and down the sides of the dunes. It is the worst possible terrain for the horses, which plod forward a few inches at a time, their hooves sinking deep in the sand. I look to our guide, but all he can do is shrug: 'It goes on for miles, we have to cross it, there is no other way.' Standing on a dune-top, shielding my eyes, staring ahead, I can see nothing but swirling sand.

That night one of the pack-horses refuses its feed. In the morning, even under the severest flogging, it will not rise. We redistribute the loads and cast away some of the firewood. While the others set out I stay behind. I can swear that the beast knows what is to happen. At the sight of the knife its eyes roll. With the blood spurting from its neck it scrambles free of the sand and totters a pace or two downwind before it falls. In extremities, I have heard, the barbarians tap their horses' veins. Will we live to regret this blood spent so lavishly on the sand?

On the seventh day, with the dunes finally behind us, we make out against the dull grey-brown of the empty landscape a strip of darker grey. From nearer we see that it stretches east and west for miles. There are even the stunted black shapes of trees. We are lucky, our guide says: there is bound to be water here.

What we have stumbled on is the bed of an ancient terminal lagoon. Dead reeds, ghostly white and brittle to the touch, line what were its banks. The trees are poplars, also long dead. They have died since the underground water receded too far to be reached by their roots years and years ago.

We unload the animals and begin to dig. At two feet we reach heavy blue clay. Beneath this there is sand again, then another stratum of clay, noticeably clammy. At a depth of seven feet, with my heart pounding and my ears ringing, I have to refuse my turn with the spade. The three men toil on, lifting the loose soil out of the pit in a tent-cloth tied at the corners.

At ten feet water begins to gather around their feet. It is sweet, there is no trace of salt, we smile with delight at each other; but it gathers very slowly and the sides of the pit have continually to be dug out as they cave in. It is only by late afternoon that we can empty out the last of our brackish lake-water and refill the waterskins. In near dark we lower the butt into our well and allow the horses to drink.

Meanwhile, now that there is an abundance of poplarwood the men have dug two little ovens back to back in the clay and built a roaring fire on top of them to bake the clay dry. When the fire abates they can rake the coals back into the ovens and set about baking bread. The girl stands watching all this, leaning on her sticks to which I have fastened discs of wood to help her in the sand. In the free and easy camaraderie of this good day, and with a day of rest promised, talk flows. Joking with her, the men make their first overture of friendship: 'Come and sit with us and taste what men's baking is like!' She smiles back at them, lifting her chin in a gesture which perhaps I alone know is an effort to see. Cautiously she sets herself down beside them to bathe in the glow from the ovens.

I myself sit further away sheltered from the wind in the mouth of my tent with one of the oil-lamps flickering beside me, making the day's entry in the log-book but listening too. The banter goes on in the pidgin of the frontier, and she is at no loss for words. I am surprised by her fluency, her quickness, her self-possession. I even catch myself in a flush of pride: she is not just the old man's slut, she is a witty, attractive young woman! Perhaps if from the beginning I had known how to use this slap-happy joking lingo with her we might have warmed more to each other. But like a fool, instead of giving her a good time I oppressed her with gloom. Truly, the world ought to belong to the singers and dancers! Futile bitterness, idle melancholy, empty regrets! I blow out the lamp, sit with my chin on my fist staring towards the fire, listening to my stomach rumble.

*

I sleep a sleep of utter exhaustion. I barely emerge into wakefulness when she lifts the edge of the huge bear-fur and snuggles against me. 'A child gets cold in the night' – that is what I think in my befuddlement, hauling her into the crook of my arm, dozing away. Perhaps for a while I am fast asleep again. Then, wide awake, I feel her hand groping under my clothes, her tongue licking my ear. A ripple of sensual joy runs through me, I yawn, stretch, and smile in the dark. Her hand finds what it is seeking. 'What of it?' I think. 'What if we perish in the middle of nowhere? Let us at least not die pinched and miserable!' Beneath her smock she is bare. With a heave I am upon her; she is warm, swollen, ready for me; in a minute five months of senseless hesitancy are wiped out and I am floating back into easy sensual oblivion.

When I wake it is with a mind washed so blank that terror rises in me. Only with a deliberate effort can I reinsert myself into time and space: into a bed, a tent, a night, a world, a body pointing west and east. Though I lie sprawled on her with the weight of a dead ox, the girl is asleep, her arms clasped slackly around my back. I ease myself off her, rearrange our covering, and try to compose myself. Not for an instant do I imagine that I can strike camp on the morrow, march back to the oasis, and in the magistrate's sunny villa set about living out my days with a young bride, sleeping placidly by her side, fathering her children, watching the seasons turn. I do not shy at the thought that if she had not spent the evening with the young men around the campfire she would very likely not have found any need for me. Perhaps the truth is that it was one of them she was embracing when I held her in my arms. I listen scrupulously to the reverberations of that thought inside me, but cannot detect a plunging of the heart to tell me I am injured. She sleeps; my hand passes back and forth over her smooth belly, caresses her thighs. It is done, I am content. At the same time I am ready to believe that it would not have been done if I were not in a few days to part from her. Nor, if I must be candid, does the pleasure I take in her, the pleasure whose distant afterglow my palm still feels, go deep. No more than before does my heart leap or my blood pound at her touch. I am with her not for whatever raptures she may promise or yield but for other reasons, which remain as obscure to me as ever. Except that it has not escaped me that in bed in the dark the marks her torturers have left upon her, the twisted feet, the half-blind eyes, are easily forgotten. Is it then the case that it is the whole woman I want, that my pleasure in her is spoiled until these marks on her are erased and she is restored to herself; or is it the case (I am not stupid, let me say these things) that it is the marks on her which drew me to her but which, to my disappointment, I find, do not go deep enough? Too much or too little: is it she I want or the traces of a history her body bears? For a long time I lie staring into what seems pitch blackness, though I know the roof of the tent is only an arm's length away. No thought that I think, no articulation, however antonymic, of the origin of my desire seems to upset me. 'I must be tired,' I think. 'Or perhaps whatever can be articulated is falsely put.' My lips move, silently composing and recomposing the words. 'Or perhaps it is the case that only that which has not been articulated has to be lived through.' I stare at this last proposition without detecting any answering movement in myself toward assent or dissent. The words grow more and more opaque before me; soon they have lost all meaning. I sigh at the end of a long day, in the middle of a long night. Then I turn to the girl, embrace her, draw her tight against me. She purrs in her sleep, where soon I have joined her.

We rest on the eighth day, for the horses are now in a truly pitiable state. They chew hungrily at the sapless fibre of the dead reed-stalks. They bloat their bellies with water and break wind massively. We have fed them the last of the linseed and even a little of our bread. Unless we find grazing in a day or two they will perish.

We leave our well behind us, and the mound of earth we dug,

to press on northwards. All of us walk except the girl. We have abandoned whatever we can afford to lighten the horses' burden; but since we cannot survive without fire they must still carry bulky loads of wood.

'When will we see the mountains?' I ask our guide.

'One day. Two days. It is hard to say. I have not travelled these parts before.' He has hunted along the eastern shore of the lake and the periphery of the desert without having reason to cross it. I wait, giving him every chance to speak his mind, but he seems unperturbed, he does not believe we are in danger. 'Perhaps two days before we see the mountains, then another day's march before we reach them.' He screws up his eyes, peering into the brown haze that veils the horizon. He does not ask what we will do when we get to the mountains.

We reach the end of this flat pebbly waste and ascend a series of rocky ridges to a low plateau, where we begin to meet with hummocks of withered winter grass. The animals tear savagely at them. It is a great relief to see them eat.

I wake up with a start in the middle of the night, filled with a dire sense that something is wrong. The girl sits up beside me: 'What is it?' she says.

'Listen. The wind has stopped.'

Barefoot, wrapped in a fur, she crawls after me out of the tent. It is snowing gently. The earth lies white on every side beneath a hazy full moon. I help her to her feet and stand holding her, staring up into the void from which the snowflakes descend, in a silence that is palpable after a week of wind beating ceaselessly in our ears. The men from the second tent join us. We smile foolishly at each other. 'Spring snow,' I say, 'the last snow of the year.' They nod. A horse shaking itself off nearby startles us.

In the snowbound warmth of the tent I make love to her again. She is passive, accommodating herself to me. When we begin I am sure that the time is right; I embrace her in the most intense pleasure and pride of life; but halfway through I seem to lose touch with her, and the act peters out vacantly. My intuitions are clearly fallible. Still, my heart continues its affectionate glow towards this girl who so briskly falls asleep in the crook of my arm. There will be another time, and if not, I do not think I mind.

A voice is calling through the slit of the tent-mouth: 'Sir, you must wake up!'

I am dazedly aware of having overslept. It is the stillness, I think to myself: it is as if we are becalmed in the stillness.

I emerge from the tent into daylight. 'Look, sir!' says the man who woke me, pointing north-east. 'Bad weather on the way!'

Rolling down upon us over the snowy plain is a gigantic black wave. It is still miles away but visibly devouring the earth in its approach. Its crest is lost in the murky clouds. 'A storm!' I shout. I have never seen anything so frightening. The men hurry to take down their tent. 'Bring the horses in, tether them here in the centre!' The first gusts are already reaching us, the snow begins to eddy and fly.

The girl is beside me on her sticks. 'Can you see it?' I say. She peers in her crooked way and nods. The men set to work striking the second tent. 'The snow was not a good sign after all!' She does not reply. Though I know I should be helping, I cannot tear my eyes from the great black wall roaring down upon us with the speed of a galloping horse. The wind rises, rocking us on our feet; the familiar howl is in our ears again.

I bestir myself. 'Quick, quick!' I call out, clapping my hands. One man is on his knees folding the tent-cloths, rolling the felts, stowing the bedclothes; the other two are bringing the horses in. 'Sit down!' I shout to the girl, and scramble to help with the packing. The storm-wall is not black any more but a chaos of whirling sand and snow and dust. Then all at once the wind rises to a scream, my cap is whirled from my head, and the storm hits us. I am knocked flat on my back: not by the wind but by a horse that breaks free and blunders about, ears flat, eyes rolling. 'Catch it!' I shout. My words are nothing but a whisper, I cannot hear them myself. The horse vanishes from sight like a phantom. At the same instant the tent is whirled high into the sky. I hurl myself upon the bundled felts, holding them down, groaning with fury at myself. Then on hands and feet, dragging the felts, I inch my way back towards the girl. It is like crawling against running water. My eyes, my nose, my mouth are already stopped with sand, I heave to breathe.

The girl stands with her arms stretched like wings over the necks of two horses. She seems to be talking to them: though their eyeballs glare, they are still.

'Our tent is gone!' I shout in her ear, waving an arm toward the sky. She turns: beneath the cap her face is wrapped in a black scarf; even her eyes are covered. 'Tent is gone!' I shout again. She nods.

For five hours we huddle behind the piled firewood and the horses while the wind lashes us with snow, ice, rain, sand, grit. We ache with cold to our very bones. The flanks of the horses, turned to the wind, are caked with ice. We press together, man and beast, sharing our warmth, trying to endure.

Then at midday the wind drops as suddenly as if a gate has been closed somewhere. Our ears ring in the unfamiliar quiet. We ought to move our numbed limbs, clean ourselves off, load the animals, anything to make the blood run in our veins, but all we want is to lie a little longer in our nest. A sinister lethargy! My voice rasps from my throat: 'Come, men, let us load.'

Humps in the sand show where our discarded baggage lies buried. We search downwind but find no sign of the lost tent. We help the creaking horses up and load them. The cold of the tempest is as nothing to the cold that succeeds it, settling like a pall of ice upon us. Our breath turns to rime, we shiver in our boots. After three unsteady seesawing steps the front horse crumples on its hindquarters. We throw aside the fire-wood it carries, lift it to its feet with a pole, whip it on. I curse myself, not for the first time, for setting out on a hard journey with an unsure guide in a treacherous season.

*

The tenth day: warmer air, clearer skies, a gentler wind. We are plodding on across the flatlands when our guide shouts and points. 'The mountains!' I think, and my heart leaps. But it is not the mountains he sees. The specks he points to in the distance are men, men on horseback: who but barbarians! I turn to the girl, whose shambling mount I lead. 'We are nearly there,' I say. 'There are people ahead, we will soon know who they are.' The oppression of the past days lifts from my shoulders. Moving to the front, quickening my pace, I turn our march towards the three tiny figures in the distance.

We push on towards them for half an hour before we realize that we are getting no closer. As we move they move too. 'They are ignoring us,' I think, and consider lighting a fire. But when I call a halt the three specks seem to halt too; when we resume our march they begin to move. 'Are they reflections of us, is this a trick of the light?' I wonder. We cannot close the gap. How long have they been dogging us? Or do they think we are dogging them?

'Stop, there is no point in chasing them,' I say to the men. 'Let us see if they will meet one of us alone.' So I mount the girl's horse and ride out alone towards the strangers. For a short while they seem to remain still, watching and waiting. Then they begin to recede, shimmering on the edge of the dust-haze. Though I urge it on, my horse is too weak to raise more than a shambling trot. I give up the chase, dismount, and wait for my companions to reach me.

To conserve the horses' strength we have been making our marches shorter and shorter. We travel no more than six miles that afternoon across firm flat terrain, the three horsemen ahead of us hovering always within eyesight, before we make camp. The horses have an hour to graze on what stunted scrubgrass they can find; then we tether them close to the tent and set a watch. Night falls, the stars come out in a hazy sky. We lounge about the campfire basking in the warmth, savouring the ache of tired limbs, reluctant to crowd into the single tent. Staring north I can swear that I glimpse the flicker of another fire; but when I try to point it out to the others the night is impenetrably black.

The three men volunteer to sleep outside, taking turns with the watch. I am touched. 'In a few days,' I say, 'when it is warmer.' We sleep fitfully, four bodies crammed together in a tent meant for two, the girl modestly outermost.

I am up before dawn staring northward. As the pinks and mauves of the sunrise begin to turn golden, the specks materialize again on the blank face of the plain, not three of them but eight, nine, ten, perhaps twelve.

With a pole and a white linen shirt I make a banner and ride out towards the strangers. The wind has dropped, the air is clear, I count as I ride: twelve tiny figures on the side of a rise, and far behind them the faintest ghostly intimation of the blue of the mountains. Then as I watch the figures begin to move. They group in a file and like ants climb the rise. On the crest they halt. A swirl of dust obscures them, then they reappear: twelve mounted men on the skyline. I plod on, the white banner flapping over my shoulder. Though I keep my eye on the crest, I fail to catch the moment at which they vanish.

'We must simply ignore them,' I tell my party. We reload and resume our march towards the mountains. Though the loads grow lighter every day, it hurts our hearts to have to flog the emaciated animals on.

The girl is bleeding, that time of the month has come for her. She cannot conceal it, she has no privacy, there is not the merest bush to hide behind. She is upset and the men are upset. It is the old story: a woman's flux is bad luck, bad for the crops, bad for the hunt, bad for the horses. They grow sullen: they want her away from the horses, which cannot be, they do not want her to touch their food. Ashamed, she keeps to herself all day and does not join us for the evening meal. After I have eaten I take a bowl of beans and dumplings to the tent where she sits.

'You should not be waiting on me,' she says. 'I should not

even be in the tent. But there is nowhere else to go.' She does not question her exclusion.

'Never mind,' I tell her. I touch my hand to her cheek, sit down for a while and watch her eat.

It is futile to press the men to sleep in the tent with her. They sleep outside, keeping the fire burning, rotating the watch. In the morning, for their sake, I go through a brief purification ceremony with the girl (for I have made myself unclean by sleeping in her bed): with a stick I draw a line in the sand, lead her across it, wash her hands and mine, then lead her back across the line into the camp. 'You will have to do the same again tomorrow morning,' she murmurs. In twelve days on the road we have grown closer than in months of living in the same rooms.

We have reached the foothills. The strange horsemen plod on far ahead of us up the winding bed of a dry stream. We have ceased trying to catch up with them. We understand now that while they are following us they are also leading us.

As the terrain grows rockier we progress more and more slowly. When we halt to rest, or lose sight of the strangers in the windings of the stream, it is without fear of their vanishing.

Then, climbing a ridge, coaxing the horses, straining and pushing and hauling, we are all of a sudden upon them. From behind the rocks, from out of a hidden gully, they emerge, men mounted on shaggy ponies, twelve and more, dressed in sheepskin coats and caps, brown-faced, weatherbeaten, narrow-eyed, the barbarians in the flesh on native soil. I am close enough to smell them where I stand: horse-sweat, smoke, half-cured leather. One of them points at my chest an ancient musket nearly as long as a man, with a dipod rest bolted near the muzzle. My heart stops. 'No,' I whisper: with elaborate caution I drop the reins of the horse I am leading and display empty hands. As slowly I turn my back, take up the reins, and, slipping and sliding on the scree, lead the horse the thirty paces down to the foot of the ridge where my companions wait.

The barbarians stand outlined against the sky above us. There is the beating of my heart, the heaving of the horses, the moan of the wind, and no other sound. We have crossed the limits of the Empire. It is not a moment to take lightly.

I help the girl from her horse. 'Listen carefully,' I say. 'I will take you up the slope and you can speak to them. Bring your sticks, the ground is loose, there is no other way up. When you have spoken you can decide what you want to do. If you want to go with them, if they will see you back to your family, go with them. If you decide to come back with us, you can come back with us. Do you understand? I am not forcing you.'

She nods. She is very nervous.

With an arm around her I help her up the pebbly slope. The barbarians do not stir. I count three of the long-barrelled muskets; otherwise they bear the short bows I am familiar with. As we reach the crest they back away slightly.

'Can you see them?' I say, panting.

She turns her head in that odd unmotivated way. 'Not well,' she says.

'Blind: what is the word for blind?'

She tells me. I address the barbarians. 'Blind,' I say, touching my eyelids. They make no response. The gun resting between the pony's ears still points at me. Its owner's eyes glint merrily. The silence lengthens.

'Speak to them,' I tell her. 'Tell them why we are here. Tell them your story. Tell them the truth.'

She looks sideways at me and gives a little smile. 'You really want me to tell them the truth?'

'Tell them the truth. What else is there to tell?'

The smile does not leave her lips. She shakes her head, keeps her silence.

'Tell them what you like. Only, now that I have brought you back, as far as I can, I wish to ask you very clearly to return to the town with me. Of your own choice.' I grip her arm. 'Do you understand me? That is what I want.'

'Why?' The word falls with deathly softness from her lips. She knows that it confounds me, has confounded me from the beginning. The man with the gun advances slowly until he is almost upon us. She shakes her head. 'No. I do not want to go back to that place.'

I scramble down the slope. 'Light a fire, brew tea, we will stop here,' I tell the men. From above, the soft cascade of the girl's speech reaches me broken by the gusting of the wind. She leans on her two sticks, the horsemen dismounting and clustering around her. I cannot make out a word. 'What a waste,' I think: 'she could have spent those long empty evenings teaching me her tongue! Too late now.'

From my saddlebag I bring out the two silver platters I have carried across the desert. I take the bolt of silk out of its wrapping. 'I would like you to have these,' I say. I guide her hand so that she can feel the softness of the silk, the chasing on the platters, fishes and leaves interlaced. I have also brought her little bundle. What it contains I do not know. I lay it on the ground. 'Will they take you all the way?'

She nods. 'He says by mid-summer. He says he wants a horse too. For me.'

'Tell him we have a long hard road before us. Our horses are in bad way, as he can see for himself. Ask if we cannot buy horses from them instead. Say we will pay in silver.'

She interprets to the old man while I wait. His companions have dismounted but he still sits his horse, the enormous old gun on its strap over his back. Stirrups, saddle, bridle, reins: no metal, but bone and fire-hardened wood sewn with gut, lashed with thongs. Bodies clothed in wool and the hides of animals and nourished from infancy on meat and milk, foreign to the suave touch of cotton, the virtues of the placid grains and fruits: these are the people being pushed off the plains into the mountains by the spread of Empire. I have never before met northerners on their own ground on equal terms: the barbarians I am familiar with are those who visit the oasis to barter, and the few who make their camp along the river, and Joll's miserable captives. What an occasion and what a shame too to be here today! One day my successors will be making collections of the artifacts of these people, arrowheads, carved knife-handles, wooden dishes, to display beside my birds' eggs and calligraphic riddles. And here I am patching up relations between the men of the future and the men of the past, returning, with apologies, a body we have sucked dry – a go-between, a jackal of Empire in sheep's clothing!

'He says no.'

I take one of the little silver bars from my bag and hold it up to him. 'Say this is for one horse.'

He leans down, takes the glittering bar, and carefully bites it; then it disappears into his coat.

'He says no. The silver is for the horse he does not take. He does not take my horse, he takes the silver instead.'

I almost lose my temper; but what good will haggling do? She is going, she is almost gone. This is the last time to look on her clearly face to face, to scrutinize the motions of my heart, to try to understand who she really is: hereafter, I know, I will begin to re-form her out of my repertoire of memories according to my questionable desires. I touch her cheek, take her hand. On this bleak hillside in mid–morning I can find no trace in myself of that stupefied eroticism that used to draw me night after night to her body or even of the comradely affection of the road. There is only a blankness, and desolation that there has to be such blankness. When I tighten my grip on her hand there is no answer. I see only too clearly what I see: a stocky girl with a broad mouth and hair cut in a fringe across her forehead staring over my shoulder into the sky; a stranger; a visitor from strange parts now on her way home after a less than happy visit. 'Goodbye,' I say. 'Goodbye,' she says. There is no more life in her voice than in mine. I begin to climb down the slope; by the time I reach the bottom they have taken the sticks from her and are helping her on to a pony.

As far as one can ever be sure, spring has come. The air is balmy, the green tips of new grass-shoots are beginning to push out here and there, flurries of desert-quail chase before us. If we had left the oasis now rather than two weeks ago we would have travelled faster and not have risked our lives. On the other hand, would we have been lucky enough to find the barbarians? This very day, I am sure, they are folding their tents, packing their carts, bringing their flocks under the whip for the spring migrations. I was not wrong to take the risk, though I know the men blame me. ('Bringing us out here in winter!' I imagine them saying. 'We should never have agreed!' And what must they think now that they realize they were not part of an embassy to the barbarians as I hinted but simply an escort for a woman, a left-over barbarian prisoner, a person of no account, the Magistrate's slut?)

We try to retrace our old route as closely as possible, relying on the star-sightings I have been careful to plot. The wind is behind us, the weather is warmer, the horses' loads are lighter, we know where we are, there is no reason why we should not travel fast. But at the first night's stop there is a setback. I am called to the campfire where one of the young soldiers sits dejectedly with his face in his hands. His boots are off, his footcloths unwrapped.

'Look at his foot, sir,' says our guide.

The right foot is puffy and inflamed. 'What is wrong?' I ask the boy. He lifts the foot and shows me a heel caked with blood and pus. Even above the smell of dirty footcloths I detect a putrid odour.

'How long has your foot been like this?' I shout. He hides his face. 'Why did you not say anything? Didn't I tell you all that you must keep your feet clean, that you must change your footcloths every second day and wash them, that you must put ointment on blisters and bandage them? I gave those orders for a reason! How are you going to travel with your foot in that condition?'

The boy does not reply. 'He did not want to hold us up,' his friend whispers.

'He did not want to hold us up but now we have to cart him all the way back!' I shout. 'Boil water, see that he cleans his foot and bandages it!'

I am right. When next morning they try to help him on with his boot he cannot hide his agony. With the bandaged foot wound in a bag and tied he can limp along over the easier ground; but for the most part he has to ride.

We will all be happy when this journey is over. We are tired of each other's company.

On the fourth day we strike the bed of the dead lagoon and follow it south-east for several miles before we reach our old waterhole with its clump of stark poplar-trunks. There we rest for a day, gathering our strength for the hardest stretch. We fry a supply of fatcakes and boil the last potful of beans to a mash.

I keep to myself. The men talk in low voices and fall into silence when I am near. All the earlier excitement has gone out of the expedition, not only because its climax has been so disappointing – a palaver in the desert followed by the same road back – but because the presence of the girl had spurred the men into sexual display, into a brotherly rivalry which has now declined into morose irritability directed willy-nilly against me for taking them on a foolhardy jaunt, against the horses for their recalcitrance, against their fellow with the sore foot for holding them up, against the brute impedimenta they have to carry, even against themselves. I set an example by laying out my bedroll beside the fire beneath the stars, preferring the cold of the open air to the choking warmth of a tent with three disgruntled men. The next night no one offers to pitch the tent and we all sleep outside.

By the seventh day we are making our way through the salt wastes. We lose another horse. The men, tired of the monotonous beans and flourcakes, ask to slaughter it for food. I give my permission but do not join in. 'I will go on ahead with the horses,' I say. Let them enjoy their feast. Let me not hinder them from imagining it is my throat they cut, my bowels they tear out, my bones they crack. Perhaps they will be friendlier afterwards.

I think with yearning of the familiar routine of my duties, of the approaching summer, the long dreamy siestas, conversations with friends at dusk under the walnut trees, with boys bringing tea and lemonade and the eligible girls in twos and threes promenading before us on the square in their finery. Only days since I parted from that other one, and I find her face hardening over in my memory, becoming opaque, impermeable, as though secreting a shell over itself. Plodding across the salt I catch myself in a moment of astonishment that I could have loved someone from so remote a kingdom. All I want now is to live out my life in ease in a familiar world, to die in my own bed and be followed to the grave by old friends.

From as far away as ten miles we can make out the jutting watchtowers against the sky; while we are still on the track south of the lake the ochre of the walls begins to separate out from the grey of the desert background. I glance at the men behind me. Their step too has quickened, they can barely hide their excitement. We have not bathed or changed our clothes in three weeks, we stink, our skin is dry and seamed in black from the beating of wind and sun, we are exhausted, but we walk like men, even the boy who stumps along now on his bandaged foot with his chest thrown out. It could have been worse: it could have been better, perhaps, but it could have been worse. Even the horses, their bellies bloated with marsh-grass, seem restored to life.

In the fields the first spring shoots are beginning to show. The thin tones of a trumpet reach our ears; the horsemen of the welcoming party issue from the gates, the sun flashing on their helmets. We look like scarecrows: it would have been better if I had told the men to put on their armour for these last few miles. I watch the horsemen trot towards us, expecting them at any moment to break into a gallop, to fire off their guns in the air and shout. But their demeanour remains businesslike, they are not a welcoming party at all, I begin to realize, there are no children running after them: they divide in two and surround us, there is not one face among them that I recognize, their eyes are stony, they do not answer my questions but march us back like prisoners through the open gates.

It is only when we emerge on to the square and see the tents and hear the hubbub that we understand: the army is here, the promised campaign against the barbarians is under way.

IV

A man sits at my desk in the office behind the courtroom. I have never seen him before but the insignia on his lilac-blue tunic tell me that he belongs to the Third Bureau of the Civil Guard. A pile of brown folders tied with pink tapes lies at his elbow; one is open before him. I recognize the folders: they contain records of taxes and levies dating back fifty years. Can he really be examining them? What is he looking for? I speak: 'Is there anything I can help you with?'

He ignores me, and the two stiff soldiers who guard me might as well be made of wood. I am far from complaining. After my weeks in the desert it is no hardship to stand idle. Besides, I sense a faraway tinge of exultation at the prospect that the false friendship between myself and the Bureau may be coming to an end.

'May I speak to Colonel Joll?' I say. A shot in the dark: who is to say that Joll has returned?

He does not answer, continuing his pretence of reading the documents. He is a good-looking man, with regular white teeth and lovely blue eyes. But vain, I think. I picture him sitting up in bed beside a girl, flexing his muscles for her, feeding on her admiration. The kind of man who drives his body like a machine, I imagine, ignorant that it has its own rhythms. When he looks at me, as he will in a moment, he will look from behind that handsome immobile face and through those clear eyes as an actor looks from behind a mask.

He looks up from the page. It is just as I thought. 'Where have you been?' he says.

'I have been away on a long journey. It pains me that I was

not here when you arrived to offer you hospitality. But now I am back, and all that is mine is yours.'

His insignia say that he is a warrant officer. Warrant Officer in the Third Bureau: what does that mean? At a guess, five years of kicking and beating people; contempt for the regular police and for due process of law; a detestation of smooth patrician talk like mine. But perhaps I do him an injustice – I have been away from the capital for a long time.

'You have been treasonously consorting with the enemy,' he says.

So it is out. 'Treasonously consorting': a phrase out of a book.

'We are at peace here,' I say, 'we have no enemies.' There is silence. 'Unless I make a mistake,' I say. 'Unless we are the enemy.'

I am not sure that he understands me. 'The natives are at war with us,' he says. I doubt that he has ever set eyes on a barbarian in his life. 'Why have you been consorting with them? Who gave you permission to leave your post?'

I shrug off the provocation. 'It is a private matter,' I say. 'You will have to take my word for that. I do not intend to discuss it. Except to say that the magistracy of a district is not a post that can be abandoned like a gatepost.'

There is a spring in my walk as I am marched away to confinement between my two guards. 'I hope you will allow me to wash,' I say, but they ignore me. Never mind.

I am aware of the source of my elation: my alliance with the guardians of the Empire is over, I have set myself in opposition, the bond is broken, I am a free man. Who would not smile? But what a dangerous joy! It should not be so easy to attain salvation. And is there any principle behind my opposition? Have I not simply been provoked into a reaction by the sight of one of the new barbarians usurping my desk and pawing my papers? As for this liberty which I am in the process of throwing away, what value does it have to me? Have I truly enjoyed the unbounded freedom of this past year in which more than ever before my life has been mine to make up as I go along? For example: my freedom to make of the girl whatever I felt like, wife or concubine or daughter or slave or all at once or none, at whim, because I had no duty to her save what it occurred to me to feel from moment to moment: from the oppression of such freedom who would not welcome the liberation of confinement? In my opposition there is nothing heroic – let me not for an instant forget that.

It is the same room in the barracks that they used for their interrogations last year. I stand by while the mats and rolls of the soldiers who have been sleeping here are dragged out and piled at the door. My own three men, still filthy and ragged, emerge from the kitchen to stare. 'What is that you are eating?' I shout. 'Get me some before they lock me up!' One of them comes trotting over with his bowl of hot millet gruel. 'Take it,' he says. The guards motion me to go in. 'Just a moment,' I say: 'let him fetch my bedroll, then I won't trouble you again.' They wait while I stand in a patch of sunlight spooning in the gruel like a starving man. The boy with the sore foot stands at my elbow with a bowl of tea, smiling. 'Thank you,' I say. 'Don't be anxious, they won't harm you, you were only doing what you were told.' With my bedroll and the old bear-fur under my arm I enter my cell. The soot-marks are still on the wall where the brazier used to stand. The door closes and darkness falls.

I sleep all day and all night, barely disturbed by the chop-chop of picks behind the wall at my head or the faraway rumble of barrows and shouts of labourers. In my dreams I am again in the desert, plodding through endless space towards an obscure goal. I sigh and wet my lips. 'What is that noise?' I ask when the guard brings my food. They are tearing down the houses built against the south wall of the barracks, he tells me: they are going to extend the barracks and build proper cells. 'Ah yes,' I say: 'time for the black flower of civilization to bloom.' He does not understand.

There is no window, only a hole high on the wall. But after a day or two my eyes have adjusted to the gloom. I have to shield myself against the light when, morning and evening, the door is flung open and I am fed. The best hour is early morning, when I wake and lie listening to the first birdsong outside, watching the square of the smokehole for the instant at which darkness gives way to the first dove-grey light.

I am fed the same rations as the common soldiers. Every second day the barracks gate is locked for an hour and I am let out to wash and exercise. There are always faces pressed against the bars of the gate gaping at the spectacle of the fall of the once mighty. Many I recognize; but no one greets me.

At night when everything is still the cockroaches come out to explore. I hear, or perhaps imagine, the horny clicking of their wings, the scurry of their feet across the paved floor. They are lured by the smell of the bucket in the corner, the morsels of food on the floor; no doubt too by this mountain of flesh giving off its multifarious odours of life and decay. One night I am awoken by the feather-light tread of one crossing my throat. Thereafter I often jerk awake during the night, twitching, brushing myself off, feeling the phantom probings of their antennae at my lips, my eyes. From such beginnings grow obsessions: I am warned.

I stare all day at the empty walls, unable to believe that the imprint of all the pain and degradation they have enclosed will not materialize under an intent enough gaze; or shut my eyes, trying to attune my hearing to that infinitely faint level at which the cries of all who suffered here must still beat from wall to wall. I pray for the day when these walls will be levelled and the unquiet echoes can finally take wing; though it is hard to ignore the sound of brick being laid on brick so nearby.

I look forward with craving to exercise times, when I can feel the wind on my face and the earth under my soles, see other faces and hear human speech. After two days of solitude my lips feel slack and useless, my own speech seems strange to me. Truly, man was not made to live alone! I build my day unreasonably around the hours when I am fed. I guzzle my food like a dog. A bestial life is turning me into a beast.

Nevertheless it is only on the empty days when I am cast wholly upon myself that I can turn seriously to the evocation

87

of the ghosts trapped between these walls of men and women who after a visit here no longer felt that they wanted to eat and could not walk unaided.

Somewhere, always, a child is being beaten. I think of one who despite her age was still a child; who was brought in here and hurt before her father's eyes; who watched him being humiliated before her, and saw that he knew what she saw.

Or perhaps by that time she could not see, and had to know by other means: the tone his voice took on when he pleaded with them to stop, for instance.

Always I find in myself this moment of shrinking from the details of what went on in here.

After that she had no father. Her father had annihilated himself, he was a dead man. It must have been at this point, when she closed herself off to him, that he threw himself upon his interrogators, if there is any truth in their story, and clawed at them like a wild animal until he was clubbed down.

I close my eyes for hours on end, sitting in the middle of the floor in the faint light of day, and try to evoke the image of that man so ill-remembered. All I see is a figure named *father* that could be the figure of any father who knows a child is being beaten whom he cannot protect. To someone he loves he cannot fulfil his duty. For this he knows he is never forgiven. This knowledge of fathers, this knowledge of condemnation, is more than he can bear. No wonder he wanted to die.

I gave the girl my protection, offering in my equivocal way to be her father. But I came too late, after she had ceased to believe in fathers. I wanted to do what was right, I wanted to make reparation: I will not deny this decent impulse, however mixed with more questionable motives: there must always be a place for penance and reparation. Nevertheless, I should never have allowed the gates of the town to be opened to people who assert that there are higher considerations than those of decency. They exposed her father to her naked and made him gibber with pain; they hurt her and he could not stop them (on a day I spent occupied with the ledgers in my office). Thereafter she was no longer fully human, sister to all of us.

Certain sympathies died, certain movements of the heart became no longer possible to her. I too, if I live long enough in this cell with its ghosts not only of the father and the daughter but of the man who even by lamplight did not remove the black discs from his eyes and the subordinate whose work it was to keep the brazier fed, will be touched with the contagion and turned into a creature that believes in nothing.

So I continue to swoop and circle around the irreducible figure of the girl, casting one net of meaning after another over her. She leans on her two sticks looking dimly upward. What does she see? The protecting wings of a guardian albatross or the black shape of a coward crow afraid to strike while its prey yet breathes?

Though the guards have orders not to discuss anything with me, it is not difficult to stitch together into a coherent story the snatches of talk I hear on my outings into the yard. All the latest talk is about the fire along the river. Five days ago it was just a darker smudge against the haze in the north-west. Since then it has eaten its way slowly down the river-course, sometimes dying down but always reviving, and clearly visible now from the town as a brown shroud over the delta where the river enters the lake.

I can guess what has happened. Someone has decided that the river-banks provide too much cover for the barbarians, that the river would form a more defensible line if the banks were cleared. So they have fired the brush. With the wind blowing from the north, the fire has spread across the whole shallow valley. I have seen wildfires before. The fire races through the reeds, the poplars flare up like torches. Animals that are quick enough – antelope, hare, cat – escape; swarms of birds fly out in terror; everything else is consumed. But there are so many barren stretches along the river that fires rarely spread. So it is clear that in this case a party must be following the fire downriver to see to its progress. They do not care that once the ground is cleared the wind begins to eat at the soil and the desert advances. Thus the expeditionary force against the barbarians prepares for its campaign, ravaging the earth, wasting our patrimony.

The shelves have been cleared, dusted and polished. The surface of the desk glows with a deep lustre, bare save for a saucer of little glass balls of different colours. The room is spotlessly clean. A vase of hibiscus flowers stands on a table in the corner filling the air with scent. There is a new carpet on the floor. My office has never looked more attractive.

I stand beside my guard in the same clothes I travelled in, my underwear washed once or twice but my coat still smelling of woodsmoke, waiting. I watch the play of sunlight through the almond-blossoms outside the window, and am content.

After a long while he enters, tosses a sheaf of papers on the desk, and sits down. He stares at me without speaking. He is trying, though somewhat too theatrically, to make a certain impression on me. The careful reorganization of my office from clutter and dustiness to this vacuous neatness, the slow swagger which he uses to cross the room, the measured insolence with which he examines me, are all meant to say something: not only that he is now in charge (how could I contest that?) but that he knows how to comport himself in an office, knows even how to introduce a note of functional elegance. Why does he think me worth the trouble of this display? Because despite my smelly clothes and my wild beard I am still from an *old family*, however contemptibly decayed out here in the back of beyond? Does he fear I will sneer unless he armours himself in a décor picked up, I have no doubt, from careful observation of the offices of his superiors in the Bureau? He will not believe me if I tell him it does not matter. I must be careful not to smile.

He clears his throat. 'I am going to read to you from the depositions we have gathered, Magistrate,' he says, 'so that you will have an idea of the gravity of the charges against you.' He motions and the guard leaves the room.

'From one: "His conduct in office left much to be desired. His decisions were characterized by arbitrariness, petitioners had on occasion to wait months for a hearing, and he maintained no regular system of accounting for moneys." ' He lays down the paper. 'I may mention that an inspection of your accounts has confirmed that there have been irregularities. "Despite being principal administrative officer for the district, he contracted a liaison with a streetwoman which occupied most of his energies, to the detriment of his official duties. The liaison had a demoralizing effect on the prestige of imperial administration because the woman in question had been patronized by the common soldiers and figured in numerous obscene stories." I will not repeat the stories.

'Let me read to you from another. "On the first of March, two weeks before the arrival of the expeditionary force, he gave orders for myself and two other men (named) to prepare at once for a long journey. He did not at that time say where we were going. We were surprised when we found that the barbarian girl would be travelling with us, but we did not ask questions. We were also surprised by the hastiness of the preparations. We did not see why we could not wait for the spring thaw. It was only after our return that we understood that his purpose had been to warn the barbarians of the coming campaign. . . . We made contact with the barbarians on approximately the eighteenth of March. He had long consultations with them from which we were excluded. An exchange of gifts also took place. At this time we discussed among ourselves what we would do if he ordered us to go over to the barbarians. We decided that we would refuse and find our own way home. . . . The girl returned to her people. He was besotted with her, but she did not care for him." '

'So.' He lays the papers down carefully and squares the corners. I keep my silence. 'I read only extracts. So that you could see the shape of things. It looks bad when we have to come in and clean up local administration. It isn't even our job.'

'I will defend myself in a court of law.'

'Will you?'

I am not surprised by what they are doing. I know very well the weight that insinuations and nuances can be made to bear or how a question can be asked in such a way as to dictate its answer. They will use the law against me as far as it serves them, then they will turn to other methods. That is the Bureau's way. To people who do not operate under statute, legal process is simply one instrument among many.

I speak. 'No one would dare to say those things to my face. Who is responsible for the first deposition?'

He waves a hand and settles back. 'Never mind. You will have your chance to reply.'

So we contemplate each other in the stillness of the morning, till it is time for him to clap his hands for the guard to remove me.

I think about him a great deal in the solitude of my cell, trying to understand his animosity, trying to see myself as he sees me. I think of the care he has spent on my office. He does not simply hurl my papers in a corner and prop his boots on my desk, but instead takes the trouble to display to me his notion of good taste. Why? A man with the waist of a boy and the muscular arms of a streetfighter crammed into the lilac-blue uniform that the Bureau has created for itself. Vain, hungry for praise, I am sure. A devourer of women, unsatisfied, unsatisfying. Who has been told that one can reach the top only by climbing a pyramid of bodies. Who dreams that one of these days he will put his foot on my throat and press. And I? I find it hard to hate him in return. The road to the top must be hard for young men without money, without patronage, with the barest of schooling, men who might as easily go into lives of crime as into the service of the Empire (but what better branch of service could they choose than the Bureau!).

Nevertheless, I am not taking easily to the humiliations of imprisonment. Sometimes, sitting on my mat staring at three specks on the wall and feeling myself drift for the thousandth time towards the questions, *Why are they in a row? Who put them there? Do they stand for anything?*, or finding as I pace the room that I am counting *one-two-three-four-five-six-one-two-three* . . ., or brushing my hand mindlessly over my face, I realize how tiny I have allowed them to make my world, how I daily become more like a beast or a simple machine, a child's spinning-wheel, for example, with eight little figures presenting themselves on the rim: father, lover, horseman, thief . . . Then I respond with movements of vertiginous terror in which I rush around the cell jerking my arms about, pulling my beard, stamping my feet, doing anything to surprise myself, to remind myself of a world beyond that is various and rich.

There are other humiliations too. My requests for clean clothes are ignored. I have nothing to wear but what I brought with me. Each exercise day, under the eye of the guard, I wash one item, a shirt or a pair of drawers, with ash and cold water, and take it back to my cell to dry (the shirt I left to dry in the yard was gone two days later). In my nostrils there is always the mouldy smell of clothing that does not see the sun.

And worse. Under the monotonous regimen of soup and porridge and tea, it has become an agony for me to move my bowels. I hesitate for days feeling stiff and bloated before I can bring myself to squat over the pail and endure the stabs of pain, the tearing of tissues that accompany these evacuations.

No one beats me, no one starves me, no one spits on me. How can I regard myself as a victim of persecution when my sufferings are so petty? Yet they are all the more degrading for their pettiness. I remember smiling when the door first closed behind me and the key turned in the lock. It seemed no great infliction to move from the solitariness of everyday existence to the solitude of a cell when I could bring with me a world of thoughts and memories. But now I begin to comprehend how rudimentary freedom is. What freedom has been left to me? The freedom to eat or go hungry; to keep my silence or gabble to myself or beat on the door or scream. If I was the object of an injustice, a minor injustice, when they locked me in here, I am now no more than a pile of blood, bone and meat that is unhappy.

My evening meal is brought by the cook's little grandson. I

am sure it puzzles him that the old Magistrate has been shut up all alone in a dark room, but he asks no questions. He enters very erect and proud, bearing the tray, while the guard holds the door open. 'Thank you,' I say, 'I'm so glad you have come, I was getting so hungry . . .' I rest my hand on his shoulder, filling the space between us with human words, while he waits gravely for me to taste and approve. 'And how is your granny today?'

'She is well, sir.'

'And the dog? Has the dog come back yet?' (From across the yard comes his grandmother's call.)

'No, sir.'

'It is spring, you know, it is the mating season: dogs go visiting, they stay away for days, then they come back without telling you where they have been. You mustn't be worried, he will come back.'

'Yes, sir.'

I taste the soup, as he wants me to do, and smack my lips. 'Say to your grandmother, thank you for the supper, it is delicious.'

'Yes, sir.' Again the call: he picks up this morning's mug and plate and prepares to go.

'And tell me: have the soldiers come back yet?' I ask quickly.

'No, sir.'

I hold the door open and stand for a moment in the doorway listening to the last twitterings of the birds in the trees under the great violet sky while the child crosses the yard with his tray. I have nothing to give him, not even a button; I have not even time to show him how to make his knuckles go click or how to catch his nose in his fist.

I am forgetting the girl. Drifting towards sleep, it comes to me with cold clarity that a whole day has passed in which I have not thought of her. Worse, I cannot remember certainly what she looks like. From her empty eyes there always seemed to be a haze spreading, a blankness that overtook all of her. I stare into the darkness waiting for an image to form; but the only memory on which I can absolutely rest is of my oiled hands sliding over her knees, her calves, her ankles. I try to recall our few intimacies but confuse them with memories of all the other warm flesh in which I have sheathed myself in the course of a lifetime. I am forgetting her, and forgetting her, I know, deliberately. Not from the moment when I stopped before her at the barracks gate and elected her have I known the root of my need for her; and now I am steadily engaged in burying her in oblivion. Cold hands, cold heart: I remember the proverb, touch my palms to my cheek, sigh in the dark.

In the dream there is someone kneeling in the shelter of the wall. The square is quite empty; the wind drives the dust in clouds; she huddles behind the collar of her coat, pulls her cap down to cover her face.

I stand over her. 'Where does it hurt?' I say. I feel the words form in my mouth, then hear them emerge thin, bodiless, like words spoken by someone else.

She brings her legs forward awkwardly and touches her ankles. She is so small that she is almost lost in the man's coat she wears. I kneel, unlace the capacious woollen socks, unwrap the bandages. The feet lie before me in the dust, disembodied, monstrous, two stranded fish, two huge potatoes.

I lift one on to my lap and begin to chafe it. Tears well from behind her eyelids and run down her cheeks. 'It is sore!' she wails in a tiny voice. 'Ssh,' I say, 'I will keep you warm.' I lift the other foot and hug the two together. The wind pours dust on us; there is grit on my teeth. I wake up with aching gums and blood in my mouth. The night is still, the moon is dark. I lie for a while looking up into blackness, then slide back into the dream.

I enter the barracks gateway and face a yard as endless as the desert. There is no hope of reaching the other side, but I plod on, carrying the girl, the only key I have to the labyrinth, her head nodding against my shoulder, her dead feet drooping on the other side.

There are other dreams in which the figure that I call *the girl* changes shape, sex, size. In one dream there are two shapes that arouse horror in me: massive and blank, they grow and grow till they fill all the space in which I sleep. I wake up choked, shouting, my throat full.

The texture of the days, on the other hand, is as dull as porridge. Never before has my nose been so rubbed in the quotidian. The flow of events in the outside world, the moral dimension of my plight, if that is what it is, a plight, even the prospect of defending myself in court, have lost all interest under the pressure of appetite and physical functions and the boredom of living one hour after another. I have caught a cold; my whole being is preoccupied in sniffing and sneezing, in the misery of being simply a body that feels itself sick and wants to be well.

One afternoon the faint irregular scrape and chink of the brick-layers' trowels on the other side of the wall suddenly ceases. Lying on my mat, I prick my ears: there is a faraway hum in the air, a faint electric quality to the still afternoon that fails to resolve itself into distinguishable sounds but leaves me tense and restless. A storm? Though I press my ear to the door I can make out nothing. The barracks yard is empty.

Later the trowels resume their chink–chink.

Towards evening the door opens and my little friend enters with my supper. I can see that he is bursting to tell me something; but the guard has come in with him and stands with a hand on his shoulder. So only his eyes speak to me: glowing with excitement, I can swear they say that the soldiers have returned. In which case why not bugles and cheering, why not horses trotting across the great square, why not the noise of preparations for a feast? Why does the guard grip the boy so tightly and whip him away before I can give him a kiss on his shaven skull? The obvious answer is that the soldiers have returned, but not in triumph. If so, I must beware.

Later in the evening there is a burst of noise from the yard and a hubbub of voices. Doors are opened and slammed, feet tramp back and forth. Some of what is said I can hear clearly: talk not of strategies or barbarian armies but of aching feet and exhaustion, an argument about sick men who must have beds. Within an hour all is quiet again. The yard is empty. Therefore there are no prisoners. That at least is cause for joy.

It is mid-morning and I have had no breakfast. I pace my room, my stomach rumbling like a hungry cow's. At the thought of salty porridge and black tea my saliva runs, I cannot help it.

Nor is there any sign that I will be let out, though this is an exercise day. The bricklayers are at work again; from the yard come sounds of everyday activity; I even hear the cook calling to her grandson. I beat on the door but no one pays any attention.

Then in mid-afternoon the key scrapes in the lock and the door opens. 'What do you want?' says my warder. 'Why have you been banging on the door?' How he must detest me! To spend days of one's life keeping watch on a closed door and attending to the animal needs of another man! He has been robbed of his freedom too, and thinks of me as the robber.

'Are you not letting me out today? I haven't had anything to eat.'

'Is that what you called me for? You'll get your food. Learn some patience. You're too fat anyway.'

'Wait. I have to empty my bucket. It stinks in here. I want to wash the floor. I want to wash my clothes too. I can't appear in front of the Colonel in clothes that smell like this. It will only bring disgrace on my warders. I need hot water and soap and a rag. Let me quickly empty my bucket and fetch hot water from the kitchen.'

My guess about the Colonel must be right, for he does not contradict me. He opens the door wider and stands aside. 'Hurry up!' he says.

There is only a scullery maid in the kitchen. She gives a start when the two of us walk in, in fact even seems about to run away. What stories have people been telling about me?

'Give him some hot water,' the guard orders. She ducks her

head and turns to the stove where there is always a great cauldron of steaming water.

Over my shoulder I say to the guard, 'A bucket – I will fetch a bucket for the water.' In a few strides I am across the kitchen to the dim recess where, along with sacks of flour and salt and crushed millet and dried peas and beans, the mops and brooms are kept. On a nail at head-height is the key to the cellar where the sides of mutton are hung. In an instant I have pocketed it. When I turn I have a wooden bucket in my hand. I hold it up while the girl ladles boiling water in. 'How are you?' I say. Her hand trembles so much that I have to take the ladle from her. 'Can I have a little soap and an old rag, please?'

Back in my cell I strip and wash in the luxuriously warm water. I wash my one spare pair of drawers, which smells like rotten onions, wring it out, hang it on the nail behind the door, and empty the bucket on the paved floor. Then I lie down to wait for nightfall.

The key turns smoothly in the lock. How many people besides myself know that the cellar key unlocks the door to my prison-room as well as the large cupboard in the main barracks-hall, that the key to the suite of rooms over the kitchen duplicates the key to the armoury door, that the key to the north-west tower stairway also opens the north-east tower stairway, the smaller cupboard in the hall, and the hatch over the waterpipe in the courtyard? One does not spend thirty years immersed in the minutiae of the life of a tiny settlement for nothing.

The stars twinkle out of a clear black sky. Through the bars of the yard gate comes the gleam of a fire on the square beyond. Beside the gate, if I strain my eyes, I can make out a dark shape, a man sitting against the wall or curled up in sleep. Does he see me in the doorway of my cell? For minutes I stand alert. He does not stir. Then I begin to edge along the wall, my bare feet making whispering noises on the patches of gravel.

I turn the corner and pass the kitchen door. The next door leads to my old apartment upstairs. It is locked. The third and last door stands open. It is the door of the little room sometimes used as a sickbay, sometimes simply to quarter men in. At a crouch, feeling with my hand before me, I creep towards the dim blue square of the barred window, fearful of stumbling over the bodies whose breathing I hear all about me.

One strand begins to separate from the skein: the sleeper at my feet breathes fast, at each exhalation giving a little moan. Is he dreaming? I pause while a few inches from me, like a machine, he continues to pant and moan in the dark. Then I creep past.

I stand at the window and look out across the town square, half expecting campfires, lines of tethered horses and stacked arms, rows of tents. But there is almost nothing to see: the embers of a single dying fire, and perhaps the gleam of two white tents far away under the trees. So the expeditionary force is not back! Or is it possible that these few souls here are all that is left of it? My heart stops at the thought. But that is not possible! These men have not been to war: at worst they have been roaming the up-river country, hunting down unarmed sheep-herders, raping their women, pillaging their homes, scattering their flocks; at best they have met no one at all – certainly not the gathered barbarian clans from whose fury the Third Bureau is engaged in protecting us.

Fingers as light as a butterfly's wing touch my ankle. I drop to my knees. 'I am thirsty,' confides a voice. It is the man who was panting. So he was not asleep.

'Quietly, my son,' I whisper. Staring, I can make out the whites of his upturned eyeballs. I touch his forehead: he is feverish. His hand comes up and grips mine. 'I have been so thirsty!' he says.

'I will bring you water,' I whisper in his ear, 'but then you must promise to be quiet. There are sick men here, they must sleep.'

The shadow beside the gate has not moved. Perhaps there is nothing there, perhaps only an old sack or a stack of firewood. I tiptoe across the gravel to the trough where the soldiers wash. The water is not clean but I cannot afford to unstop the pipe.

A battered pot hangs at the side of the trough. I scoop it full and tiptoe back.

The boy tries to sit up but is too weak. I support him while he drinks.

'What happened?' I whisper. One of the other sleepers stirs. 'Are you hurt or are you sick?'

'I'm so hot!' he groans. He wants to throw his blanket aside but I restrain him. 'You must sweat the fever out,' I whisper. He shakes his head slowly from side to side. I hold his wrist till he sinks back into sleep.

There are three bars set in a wooden frame: all the downstairs windows of the barracks block are barred. I brace my foot against the frame, grip the middle bar, and heave. I sweat and strain, there is a stab of pain in my back, but the bar does not budge. Then all of a sudden the frame cracks and I have to cling to prevent myself from falling backwards. The boy begins moaning again, another sleeper clears his throat. I almost shout with surprise at the pain that comes when I put my weight on my right leg.

The window itself is open. Forcing the bars to one side, I push my head and shoulders through the gap, work my way out, and tumble to earth at last behind the row of cropped bushes that runs along the north wall of the barracks. All I can think of is the pain, all that I desire is to be left to lie in the easiest position I can find, on my side with my knees raised toward my chin. For an hour at least, while I could be pursuing my escape, I lie there, hearing through the open window the sighs of the sleepers, the voice of the boy mumbling to himself. The last embers of the fire on the square die. Man and beast are asleep. It is the hour before dawn, the coldest hour. I feel the chill of the earth enter my bones. If I lie here longer I will freeze and be trundled back to my cell in the morning in a barrow. Like a wounded snail I begin to creep along the wall towards the dark mouth of the first street leading off the square.

The gate to the little area behind the inn lies back rotten on its hinges. The area itself smells of decay. Peelings, bones, slops, ash are hurled out here from the kitchen to be forked into the ground; but the earth has grown tired, the fork that buries this week's refuse turns up last week's. During the day the air is alive with flies; at dusk the blackbeetle and cockroach wake.

Beneath the wooden stairway that leads up to the balcony and servants' quarters is a recess where wood is stored and where the cats retire when it rains. I crawl in and curl up on an old bag. It smells of urine, it is certainly full of fleas, I am so cold that my teeth chatter; but at this moment all that occupies me is the palliation of the pain in my back.

I am woken by a clatter of footsteps on the stairway. It is daylight: confused, thick-headed, I cower back in my den. Someone opens the kitchen door. From all corners chickens come scurrying. It is only a matter of time before I am discovered.

As boldly as I can, but wincing despite myself, I mount the stairs. How must I look to the world with my dingy shirt and trousers, my bare feet, my unkempt beard? Like a domestic, I pray, an ostler come home after a night's carousing.

The passageway is empty, the door to the girl's room open. The room is neat and tidy as ever: the fleecy skin on the floor beside the bed, the red chequered curtain drawn over the window, the kist pushed against the far wall with a rack of clothes above it. I bury my face in the fragrance of her clothes and think of the little boy who brought my food, of how when my hand rested on his shoulder I would feel the healing power of the touch run through a body grown stiff with unnatural solitude.

The bed is made up. When I slip my hand between the sheets I imagine I can feel the faint afterglow of her warmth. Nothing would please me more than to curl up in her bed, lay my head on her pillow, forget my aches and pains, ignore the hunt that must by now have been launched for me, and like the little girl in the story tumble into oblivion. How voluptuously I feel the attraction of the soft, the warm, the odorous this morning! With a sigh I kneel and coax my body in under the bed. Face down, pressed so tightly between the floor and the slats of the bed that when I move my shoulders the bed lifts, I try to compose myself for a day in hiding.

I doze and wake, drifting from one formless dream to another. By mid-morning it has become too hot to sleep. As long as I can, I lie sweating in my close dusty retreat. Then, though I postpone it, the time comes when I have to relieve myself. Groaning I inch my way out and squat over the chamberpot. Again the pain, the tearing. I dab myself with a filched white handkerchief, which comes away bloody. The room stinks: even I, who have been living for weeks with a slop pail in the corner, am disgusted. I open the door and hobble down the passageway. The balcony looks over rows of roofs, then beyond them over the south wall and the desert stretching into the blue distance. There is no one to be seen except a woman on the other side of the alleyway sweeping her step. A child crawls on hands and knees behind her pushing something in the dust, I cannot see what. Its neat little bottom points up in the air. As the woman turns her back I step out of the shadows and hurl the contents of the pot out on to the refuse-heap below. She notices nothing.

A torpor is already beginning to settle over the town. The morning's work is over: anticipating the heat of midday, people are retiring to their shaded courtyards or to the cool green of inner rooms. The babble of water in the street-furrows dies down and stops. All I can hear is the clink of the farrier's hammer, the cooing of turtledoves, and somewhere far away the wail of a baby.

Sighing I lay myself down on the bed in the sweet remembered scent of flowers. How inviting to join the rest of the town in its siesta! These days, these hot spring days already becoming summer – how easy I find it to slip into their languorous mood! How can I accept that disaster has overtaken my life when the world continues to move so tranquilly through its cycles? It takes no effort to believe that when the shadows begin to lengthen and the first breath of wind stirs the leaves, I will wake up and yawn and dress and descend the stairs and cross the square to my office, nodding to the friends and neighbours I pass, that I will spend an hour or two there, tidy my desk, lock up, that everything will go on being as it has always been. I must actually shake my head and blink my eyes to realize that as I lie here I am a hunted man, that in the course of their duty soldiers are going to come here and haul me away and lock me up again out of the sight of the sky and of other human beings. '*Why*?' I groan into the pillow: '*Why me*?' Never has there been anyone so confused and innocent of the world as I. A veritable baby! Yet if they can they will shut me away to moulder, subject my body to their intermittent vile attentions, then one day without warning fetch me out and rush me through one of the closed trials they conduct under the emergency powers, with the stiff little colonel presiding and his henchman reading the charges and two junior officers as assessors to lend the proceedings an air of legality in an otherwise empty courtroom; and then, particularly if they have suffered reverses, particularly if the barbarians have humiliated them, they will find me guilty of treason — need I doubt that? From the courtroom to the executioner they will drag me kicking and weeping, bewildered as the day I was born, clinging to the end to the faith that no harm can come to the guiltless. 'You are living in a dream!' I say to myself: I pronounce the words aloud, stare at them, try to grasp their significance: 'You must wake up!' Deliberately I bring to mind images of innocents I have known: the boy lying naked in the lamplight with his hands pressed to his groins, the barbarian prisoners squatting in the dust, shading their eyes, waiting for whatever is to come next. Why should it be inconceivable that the behemoth that trampled them will trample me too? I truly believe I am not afraid of death. What I shrink from, I believe, is the shame of dying as stupid and befuddled as I am.

There is a flurry of voices, men's and women's, from the yard below. As I scuttle into my hiding-place I hear the tramp of footsteps on the stairs. They recede to the far end of the balcony, then come slowly back, pausing at each door. The walls separating the cubicles on this upper floor where the servants sleep and where a soldier of the garrison can buy a night's privacy are mere slats papered over: I can hear clearly as my hunter throws open each door in turn. I press myself against the wall. I hope he does not smell me.

The footsteps round the corner and come down the passage. My door is opened, held open for a few seconds, closed again. So I have passed one test.

There is a quicker, lighter tread: someone runs down the passage and enters the room. My head is turned the wrong way, I cannot even see her feet, but I know it is the girl. This is the moment at which I ought to come into the open, beg her to hide me till night falls and I can find my way out of the town and down to the lakeside. But how can I do it? By the time the bed has stopped heaving and I have emerged she will have fled screaming for help. And who is to say that she would offer refuge to one of the many men who have spent time in this room, one of many passing men from whom she earns a livelihood, a man in disgrace, a fugitive? Would she even recognize me as I am? Her feet flutter about the room, stopping here, stopping there. I can make out no pattern in their movements. I lie still, breathing softly, sweat dripping off me. All at once she is gone: the stairs creak, there is silence.

A lull falls over me too, a spell of lucidity in which I see how ridiculous it is, all this running and hiding, what a silly thing it is to be lying under a bed on a hot afternoon waiting for a chance to sneak away to the reed-brakes, there to live no doubt on birds' eggs and fish that I catch with my hands, sleeping in a hole in the earth, biding my time till this phase of history grinds past and the frontier returns to its old somnolence. The truth is that I am not myself, I have been terror-stricken, I perceive, since the moment in my cell when I saw the guard's fingers clamp over the shoulder of the little boy to remind him not to speak to me, and knew that, whatever it was that had happened that day, I was to bear the blame for it. I walked into that cell a sane man sure of the rightness of my cause, however incompetent I continue to find myself to describe what that cause may be; but after two months among the cockroaches with nothing to see but four walls and an enigmatic soot-mark, nothing to smell but the stench of my own body, no one to talk to but a ghost in a dream whose lips seem to be sealed, I am much less sure of myself. The craving to touch and be touched by another human body sometimes comes over me with such force that I groan; how I looked forward to the single brief contact which was all I could have with the boy, morning and evening! To lie in a woman's arms in a proper bed, to have good food to eat, to walk in the sun – how much more important these seem than the right to decide without advice from the police who should be my friends and who my enemies! How can I be in the right when there is not a soul in the town who approves of my escapade with the barbarian girl or who would not feel bitter against me if young men from here were killed by my barbarian protégés? And what is the point of suffering at the hands of the men in blue if I am not iron-hard in my certainty? No matter if I told my interrogators the truth, recounted every word I uttered on my visit to the barbarians, no matter even if they were tempted to believe me, they would press on with their grim business, for it is an article of faith with them that the last truth is told only in the last extremity. I am running away from pain and death. I have no plan of escape. Hiding away in the reeds I would starve within a week, or be smoked out. I am simply seeking ease, if the truth be told, fleeing to the only soft bed and friendly arms I have left to me.

Again footsteps. I recognize the girl's quick tread, this time not alone but with a man. They enter the room. By his voice he cannot be more than a boy. 'You shouldn't let them treat you like that! You're not their slave!' he says with vehemence.

'You don't understand,' she replies. 'Anyway, I don't want to talk about it now.' There is silence, then more intimate sounds.

I flush. It is intolerable that I should stay for this. Yet like the cuckold in the farce I hold my breath, sinking further and further into disgrace.

One of them sits down on the bed. Boots thud to the floor, clothes rustle, two bodies stretch themselves out an inch above me. The slats bow, pressing into my back. I stop my ears, ashamed to listen to the words they say to each other, but cannot prevent myself from hearing the fluttering and moaning I remember so well from the girl in the grip of pleasure, the girl I used to have my own endearments for.

The slats press harder upon me, I flatten myself as far as I can, the bed begins to creak. Sweating, flushed, sickened to feel how aroused I am despite myself, I actually groan: the long low groan curls from my throat and mingles unnoticed with the sounds of their panting breath.

Then it is over. They sigh and subside, the twitchings and stirrings cease, they lie at rest side by side drifting off into sleep, while unhappy, rigid, wide awake, I wait my chance to escape. It is the hour when even the chickens doze, the hour when there is only one emperor, the sun. The heat in this tiny room under the flat roof has grown stifling. I have not eaten or drunk all day.

Pushing with my feet against the wall, I edge out till I can gingerly sit up. The pain in my back, an old man's pain, announces itself again. 'I am sorry,' I whisper. They are truly asleep, like children, a boy and a girl, naked, hand in hand, beaded with sweat, their faces relaxed and oblivious. The tide of shame sweeps over me with redoubled force. Her beauty awakes no desire in me: instead it seems more obscene than ever that this heavy slack foul-smelling old body (how could they not have noticed the smell?) should ever have held her in its arms. What have I been doing all this time, pressing myself upon such flowerlike soft-petalled children – not only on her, on the other one too? I should have stayed among the gross and decaying where I belong: fat women with acrid armpits and bad tempers, whores with big slack cunts. I tiptoe out, hobble down the stairs in the blinding glare of the sun.

The upper flap of the kitchen door stands open. An old woman, bent and toothless, stands eating out of a cast-iron pot. Our eyes meet; she stops, the spoon in mid-air, her mouth open. She recognizes me. I raise a hand and smile – I am surprised at how easily the smile comes. The spoon moves, the lips close over it, her gaze shifts, I pass on.

The north gate is closed and barred. I climb the stairway to the watchtower over the angle of the wall and stare out hungrily over the beloved landscape: the belt of green stretching along the river, blackened now in patches; the lighter green of the marshes where the new reeds are shooting; the dazzling surface of the lake.

But there is something wrong. How long have I been locked away from the world, two months or ten years? The young wheat in the acres below the wall ought by now to be a vigorous eighteen inches high. It is not: except at the western limit of the irrigated area the young plants are a stunted sickly yellow. There are great bare patches nearer the lake, and a line of grey stooks by the irrigation wall.

Before my eyes the neglected fields, the sunstruck square, the empty streets shift into a new and sinister configuration. The town is being abandoned — what else is there to suppose? — and the noises I heard two nights ago must have been noises not of arrival but of departure! My heart lurches (with horror? with gratitude?) at the thought. Yet I must be mistaken: when I look down more carefully at the square I can see two boys quietly playing marbles under the mulberry trees; and from what I have seen of the inn, life is going on as usual.

In the south-west tower a sentry sits on his high stool staring vacantly into the desert. I am within a pace of him before he notices me and starts.

'Get down,' he says in a flat voice, 'you are not allowed up here.' I have never seen him before. Since I left my cell, I realize, I have not seen one of the soldiers who made up the old garrison. Why are there only strangers around?

'Don't you know me?' I say.

'Get down.'

'I will, but first I have a very important question to ask you. You see, there is no one to ask but you — everyone else seems to be asleep or away. What I want to ask is: Who are you? Where is everyone I used to know? What has happened out there in the fields? It looks as though there has been a washaway. But why should there be a washaway?' His eyes narrow as I gabble on. 'I am sorry to ask such stupid questions, but I have had a fever, I have been confined to bed' – the quaint phrase comes unbidden – 'and today is the first day I have been allowed to get up. That is why . . .'

'You must be careful of the midday sun, father,' he says. His ears stick out under a cap that is too large for him. 'You would be better off resting at this time of day.'

'Yes . . . Do you mind if I have some water?' He passes me his flask and I drink the lukewarm water, trying not to betray how savage my thirst is. 'But tell me, what has happened?'

'Barbarians. They cut away part of the embankment over there and flooded the fields. No one saw them. They came in the night. The next morning it was like a second lake.' He has stuffed his pipe, now he offers it to me. Courteously I decline ('I will only begin coughing, and that is bad for me'). 'Yes, the farmers are very unhappy. They say the crop is ruined and it is too late to plant again.'

'That's bad. It means a hard winter ahead. We will have to draw our belts very tight.'

'Yes, I don't envy you people. They could do it again, couldn't they, the barbarians. They could flood these fields any time they chose to.'

We discuss the barbarians and their treachery. They never stand up and fight, he says: their way is to creep up behind you and stick a knife in your back. 'Why can't they leave us alone? They have their own territories, haven't they?' I turn the conversation to the old days when everything used to be quiet on the frontier. He calls me 'father', which is his peasant's way of showing respect, and listens to me as one listens to mad old folk, anything being better, I suppose, than staring out into emptiness all day.

'Tell me,' I say: 'two nights ago I heard horsemen and thought the big expedition had returned.'

'No,' he laughs, 'those were just a few men they sent back. They sent them in one of the big carts. That must have been what you heard. They fell sick from the water – bad water out there, I hear – so they sent them back.'

'I see! I couldn't understand what it was. But when do you expect the main force back?'

'Soon, it must be soon. You can't live on the fruit of the land out here, can you? I've never seen such dead country.'

I climb down the steps. Our conversation has left me feeling almost venerable. Strange that no one warned him to watch out for a fat old man in ragged clothes! Or has he perhaps been perched up there since last night with no one to speak to? Who would have thought I could lie so blandly! It is mid-afternoon. My shadow glides beside me like a pool of ink. I seem to be the only creature within these four walls that moves. I am so elated that I want to sing. Even my sore back has ceased to matter.

I open the small side gate and pass out. My friend in the watchtower looks down at me. I wave, and he waves back. 'You will need a hat!' he calls. I pat my bare skull, shrug, smile. The sun beats down.

The spring wheat is indeed ruined. Warm ochre mud squelches between my toes. In places there are still puddles. Many of the young plants have been washed right out of the ground. All show a yellowish discoloration of leaf. The area nearest the lake is the worst hit. Nothing is left standing, indeed the farmers have already begun to stack the dead plants for burning. In the far fields a rise of a few inches in elevation has made all the difference. So perhaps a quarter of the planting can be saved.

The earthwork itself, the low mud wall that runs for nearly two miles and keeps the lake-water in check when it rises to its summer limit, has been repaired, but almost the whole of the intricate system of channels and gates that distributes the water around the fields has been washed away. The dam and waterwheel by the lakeshore are unharmed, though there is no sign of the horse that usually turns the wheel. I can see that weeks of hard work await the farmers. And at any moment their work can be brought to nothing by a few men armed with spades! How can we win such a war? What is the use of textbook military operations, sweeps and punitive raids into the enemy's heartland, when we can be bled to death at home?

I take the old road that curves behind the west wall before petering out into a track that leads nowhere but to the sand-filled ruins. Are the children still allowed to play there, I wonder, or do their parents keep them at home with stories of barbarians lurking in the hollows? I glance up at the wall; but my friend in the tower seems to have gone to sleep.

All the excavation we did last year has been undone by driftsand. Only corner-posts stand out here and there in the desolation where, one must believe, people once lived. I scour a hollow for myself and sit down to rest. I doubt that anyone would come looking for me here. I could lean against this ancient post with its faded carvings of dolphins and waves and be blistered by the sun and dried by the wind and eventually frozen by the frost, and not be found until in some distant era of peace the children of the oasis come back to their playground and find the skeleton, uncovered by the wind, of an archaic desert-dweller clad in unidentifiable rags.

I wake up chilled. The sun rests huge and red upon the western horizon. The wind is rising: already flying sand has banked up against my side. I am conscious above all of thirst. The plan I have toyed with, of spending the night here among the ghosts, shivering with cold, waiting for the familiar walls and treetops to materialize again out of the dark, is insupportable. There is nothing for me outside the walls but to starve. Scuttling from hole to hole like a mouse I forfeit even the appearance of innocence. Why should I do my enemies' work for them? If they want to spill my blood, let them at least bear the guilt of it. The gloomy fear of the past day has lost its force. Perhaps this escapade has not been futile if I can recover, however dimly, a spirit of outrage.

I rattle the gate of the barracks yard. 'Don't you know who is here? I've had my holiday, now let me back in!'

Someone comes running up: in the dim light we peer at each other through the bars: it is the man assigned as my warder. 'Be quiet!' he whispers through his teeth, and tugs at the bolts. Behind him voices murmur, people gather.

Gripping my arm he takes me at a trot across the yard. 'Who is it?' someone calls. It is on the tip of my tongue to reply, to take the key out and wave it, when it strikes me that this act might be imprudent. So I wait at my old door till my warder unlocks it, pushes me inside, and closes it on the two of us. His voice comes to me out of the darkness tight with anger: 'Listen: you talk to anyone about getting out and I'll make your life a misery! You understand? I'll make you pay! You say nothing! If anyone asks you about this evening, say I took you out for a walk, for exercise, nothing more. Do you understand me?'

I unpick his fingers from my arm and slide away from him. 'You see how easy it would be for me to run away and seek shelter with the barbarians,' I murmur. 'Why do you think I came back? You are only a common soldier, you can only obey orders. Still: think about it.' He clutches my wrist, and again I loosen his fingers. 'Think about why I came back and what it would have meant if I had not. You can't expect sympathy from the men in blue, I'm sure you know that. Think what might happen if I got out again.' Now I grip his hand. 'But don't fret, I won't talk: make up any story you like and I will support you. I know what it is like to be frightened.' There is a long suspicious silence. 'Do you know what I want most of all?' I say. 'I want something to eat and something to drink. I am starved, I have had nothing all day.'

So all is as it was before. This absurd incarceration continues. I lie on my back watching the block of light above me growing stronger and then weaker day after day. I listen to the remote sounds of the bricklayer's trowel, the carpenter's hammer coming through the wall. I eat and drink and, like everyone else, I wait.

First there is the sound of muskets far away, as diminutive as popguns. Then from nearer by, from the ramparts themselves, come volleys of answering shots. There is a stampede of footsteps across the barracks yard. 'The barbarians!' someone shouts; but I think he is wrong. Above all the clamour the great bell begins to peal.

Kneeling with an ear to the crack of the door I try to make out what is going on.

The noise from the square mounts from a hubbub to a steady roar in which no single voice can be distinguished. The whole town must be pouring out in welcome, thousands of ecstatic souls. Volleys of musket-shots keep cracking. Then the tenor of the roar changes, rises in pitch and excitement. Faintly above it come the brassy tones of bugles.

The temptation is too great. What have I to lose? I unlock the door. In glare so blinding that I must squint and shade my eyes, I cross the yard, pass through the gate, and join the rear of the crowd. The volleys and the roar of applause continue. The old woman in black beside me takes my arm to steady herself and stands on her toes. 'Can you see?' she says. 'Yes, I can see men on horseback,' I reply; but she is not listening.

I can see a long file of horsemen who, amid flying banners, pass through the gateway and make their way to the centre of the square where they dismount. There is a cloud of dust over the whole square, but I see that they are smiling and laughing: one of them rides with his hands raised high in triumph, another waves a garland of flowers. They progress slowly, for the crowd presses around them, trying to touch them, throwing flowers, clapping their hands above their heads in joy, spinning round and round in private ecstasies. Children dive past me, scrambling through the legs of the grownups to be nearer to their heroes. Fusillade after fusillade comes from the ramparts, which are lined with cheering people.

One part of the cavalcade does not dismount. Headed by a stern-faced young corporal bearing the green and gold banner of the battalion, it passes through the press of bodies to the far end of the square and then begins a circuit of the perimeter, the crowd surging slowly in its wake. The word runs like fire from neighbour to neighbour: '*Barbarians!*'

The standard-bearer's horse is led by a man who brandishes a heavy stick to clear his way. Behind him comes another trooper trailing a rope; and at the end of the rope, tied neck to neck, comes a file of men, barbarians, stark naked, holding their hands up to their faces in an odd way as though one and all are suffering from toothache. For a moment I am puzzled by the posture, by the tiptoeing eagerness with which they follow their leader, till I catch a glint of metal and at once comprehend. A simple loop of wire runs through the flesh of each man's hands and through holes pierced in his cheeks. 'It makes them meek as lambs,' I remember being told by a soldier who had once seen the trick: 'they think of nothing but how to keep very still.' My heart grows sick. I know now that I should not have left my cell.

I have to turn my back smartly to avoid being seen by the two who, with their mounted escort, bring up the rear of the procession: the bareheaded young captain whose first triumph this is, and at his shoulder, leaner and darker after his months of campaigning, Colonel of Police Joll.

The circuit is made, everyone has a chance to see the twelve miserable captives, to prove to his children that the barbarians are real. Now the crowd, myself reluctantly in its wake, flows towards the great gate, where a half-moon of soldiers blocks its way until, compressed at front and rear, it cannot budge.

'What is going on?' I ask my neighbour.

'I don't know,' he says, 'but help me to lift him.' I help him to lift the child he carries on his arm on to his shoulders. 'Can you see?' he asks the child.

'Yes.'

'What are they doing?'

'They are making those barbarians kneel. What are they going to do to them?'

'I don't know. Let's wait and see.'

Slowly, titanically, with all my might, I turn and begin to squeeze my body out. 'Excuse me . . . excuse me . . .' I say: 'the heat – I'm going to be sick.' For the first time I see heads turn, fingers point.

I ought to go back to my cell. As a gesture it will have no effect, it will not even be noticed. Nevertheless, for my own sake, as a gesture to myself alone, I ought to return to the cool dark and lock the door and bend the key and stop my ears to the noise of patriotic bloodlust and close my lips and never speak again. Who knows, perhaps I do my fellow-townsmen an injustice, perhaps at this very minute the shoemaker is at home tapping on his last, humming to himself to drown the shouting, perhaps there are housewives shelling peas in their kitchens, telling stories to occupy their restless children, perhaps there are farmers still going calmly about the repair of the ditches. If comrades like these exist, what a pity I do not know them! For me, at this moment, striding away from the crowd, what has become important above all is that I should neither be contaminated by the atrocity that is about to be committed nor poison myself with impotent hatred of its perpetrators. I cannot save the prisoners, therefore let me save myself. Let it at the very least be said, if it ever comes to be said, if there is ever anyone in some remote future interested to know the way we lived, that in this farthest outpost of the Empire of light there existed one man who in his heart was not a barbarian.

I pass through the barracks gate into my prison yard. At the trough in the middle of the yard I pick up an empty bucket and fill it. With the bucket held up before me, slopping water over its sides, I approach the rear of the crowd again. 'Excuse me,' I say, and push. People curse me, give way, the bucket tilts and splashes, I forge forward till in a minute I am suddenly clear in the frontmost rank of the crowd behind the backs of the soldiers who, holding staves between them, keep an arena clear for the exemplary spectacle.

Four of the prisoners kneel on the ground. The other eight, still roped together, squat in the shade of the wall watching, their hands to their cheeks.

The kneeling prisoners bend side by side over a long heavy pole. A cord runs from the loop of wire through the first man's mouth, under the pole, up to the second man's loop, back under the pole, up to the third loop, under the pole, through the fourth loop. As I watch a soldier slowly pulls the cord tighter and the prisoners bend further till finally they are kneeling with their faces touching the pole. One of them writhes his shoulders in pain and moans. The others are silent, their thoughts wholly concentrated on moving smoothly with the cord, not giving the wire a chance to tear their flesh.

Directing the soldier with little gestures of the hand is Colonel Joll. Though I am only one in a crowd of thousands, though his eyes are shaded as ever, I stare at him so hard with a face so luminous with query that I know at once he sees me.

Behind me I distinctly hear the word *magistrate*. Do I imagine it or are my neighbours inching away from me?

The Colonel steps forward. Stooping over each prisoner in turn he rubs a handful of dust into his naked back and writes a word with a stick of charcoal. I read the words upside down: ENEMY . . . ENEMY . . . ENEMY . . . ENEMY. He steps back and folds his hands. At a distance of no more than twenty paces he and I contemplate each other.

Then the beating begins. The soldiers use the stout green cane staves, bringing them down with the heavy slapping sounds of washing-paddles, raising red welts on the prisoners' backs and buttocks. With slow care the prisoners extend their legs until they lie flat on their bellies, all except the one who had been moaning and who now gasps with each blow.

The black charcoal and ochre dust begin to run with sweat and blood. The game, I see, is to beat them till their backs are washed clean.

I watch the face of a little girl who stands in the front rank of the crowd gripping her mother's clothes. Her eyes are round, her thumb is in her mouth: silent, terrified, curious, she drinks in the sight of these big naked men being beaten. On every face around me, even those that are smiling, I see the same expression: not hatred, not bloodlust, but a curiosity so intense that their bodies are drained by it and only their eyes live, organs of a new and ravening appetite.

The soldiers doing the beating grow tired. One stands with his hands on his hips panting, smiling, gesturing to the crowd. There is a word from the Colonel: all four of them cease their labour and come forward offering their canes to the spectators.

A girl, giggling and hiding her face, is pushed forward by her friends. 'Go on, don't be afraid!' they urge her. A soldier puts a cane in her hand and leads her to the place. She stands confused, embarrassed, one hand still over her face. Shouts, jokes, obscene advice are hurled at her. She lifts the cane, brings it down smartly on the prisoner's buttocks, drops it, and scuttles to safety to a roar of applause.

There is a scramble for the canes, the soldiers can barely keep order, I lose sight of the prisoners on the ground as people press forward to take a turn or simply watch the beating from nearer. I stand forgotten with my bucket between my feet.

Then the flogging is over, the soldiers reassert themselves, the crowd scrambles back, the arena is reconstituted, though narrower than before.

Over his head, exhibiting it to the crowd, Colonel Joll holds a hammer, an ordinary four-pound hammer used for knocking in tent-pegs. Again his gaze meets mine. The babble subsides.

'No!' I hear the first word from my throat, rusty, not loud enough. Then again: 'No!' This time the word rings like a bell from my chest. The soldier who blocks my way stumbles aside. I am in the arena holding up my hands to still the crowd: 'No! No! No!'

When I turn to Colonel Joll he is standing not five paces from me, his arms folded. I point a finger at him. 'You!' I shout. Let it all be said. Let him be the one on whom the anger breaks. 'You are depraving these people!'

He does not flinch, he does not reply.

'You!' My arm points at him like a gun. My voice fills the square. There is utter silence; or perhaps I am too intoxicated to hear.

Something crashes into me from behind. I sprawl in the dust, gasp, feel the sear of old pain in my back. A stick thuds down on me. Reaching out to ward it off, I take a withering blow on my hand.

It becomes important to stand up, however difficult the pain makes it. I come to my feet and see who it is that is hitting me. It is the stocky man with the sergeant's stripes who helped with the beatings. Crouched at the knees, his nostrils flaring, he stands with his stick raised for the next blow. 'Wait!' I gasp, holding out my limp hand. 'I think you have broken it!' He strikes, and I take the blow on the forearm. I hide my arm, lower my head, and try to grope towards him and grapple. Blows fall on my head and shoulders. Never mind: all I want is a few moments to finish what I am saying now that I have begun. I grip his tunic and hug him to me. Though he wrestles, he cannot use his stick; over his shoulder I shout again.

'Not with that!' I shout. The hammer lies cradled in the Colonel's folded arms. 'You would not use a hammer on a beast, not on a beast!' In a terrible surge of rage I turn on the sergeant and hurl him from me. Godlike strength is mine. In a minute it will pass: let me use it well while it lasts! 'Look!' I shout. I point to the four prisoners who lie docilely on the earth, their lips to the pole, their hands clasped to their faces like monkeys' paws, oblivious of the hammer, ignorant of what is going on behind them, relieved that the offending mark has been beaten from their backs, hoping that the punishment is at an end. I raise my broken hand to the sky. 'Look!' I shout. 'We are the great miracle of creation! But from some blows this miraculous body cannot repair itself! How – !' Words fail me. 'Look at these men!' I recommence. '*Men!*' Those in the crowd who can crane to look at the prisoners, even at the flies that begin to settle on their bleeding welts.

I hear the blow coming and turn to meet it. It catches me full across the face. 'I am blind!' I think, staggering back into the blackness that instantly falls. I swallow blood; something blooms across my face, starting as a rosy warmth, turning to fiery agony. I hide my face in my hands and stamp around in a circle trying not to shout, trying not to fall.

What I wanted to say next I cannot remember. A miracle of

creation – I pursue the thought but it eludes me like a wisp of smoke. It occurs to me that we crush insects beneath our feet, miracles of creation too, beetles, worms, cockroaches, ants, in their various ways.

I take my fingers from my eyes and a grey world re-emerges swimming in tears. I am so profoundly grateful that I cease to feel pain. As I am hustled, a man at each elbow, back through the murmuring crowd to my cell, I even find myself smiling.

That smile, that flush of joy, leave behind a disturbing residue. I know that they commit an error in treating me so summarily. For I am no orator. What would I have said if they had let me go on? That it is worse to beat a man's feet to pulp than to kill him in combat? That it brings shame on everyone when a girl is permitted to flog a man? That spectacles of cruelty corrupt the hearts of the innocent? The words they stopped me from uttering may have been very paltry indeed, hardly words to rouse the rabble. What, after all, do I stand for besides an archaic code of gentlemanly behaviour towards captured foes, and what do I stand against except the new science of degradation that kills people on their knees, confused and disgraced in their own eyes? Would I have dared to face the crowd to demand justice for these ridiculous barbarian prisoners with their backsides in the air? *Justice*: once that word is uttered, where will it all end? Easier to shout *No!* Easier to be beaten and made a martyr. Easier to lay my head on a block than to defend the cause of justice for the barbarians: for where can that argument lead but to laying down our arms and opening the gates of the town to the people whose land we have raped? The old magistrate, defender of the rule of law, enemy in his own way of the State, assaulted and imprisoned, impregnably virtuous, is not without his own twinges of doubt.

My nose is broken, I know, and perhaps also the cheekbone where the flesh was laid open by the blow of the stick. My left eye is swelling shut.

As the numbness wears off the pain begins to come in spasms a minute or two apart so intense that I can no longer lie still. At the height of the spasm I trot around the room holding my face, whining like a dog; in the blessed valleys between the peaks I breathe deeply, trying to keep control of myself, trying not to make too disgraceful an outcry. I seem to hear surges and lulls in the noise from the mob on the square but cannot be sure that the roar is not simply in my eardrums.

They bring me my evening meal as usual but I cannot eat. I cannot keep still, I have to walk back and forth or rock on my haunches to keep myself from screaming, tearing my clothes, clawing my flesh, doing whatever people do when the limit of their endurance is reached. I weep, and feel the tears stinging the open flesh. I hum the old song about the rider and the juniper bush over and over again, clinging to the remembered words even after they have ceased to make any sense. One, two, three, four . . . I count. It will be a famous victory, I tell myself, if you can last the night.

In the early hours of the morning, when I am so giddy with exhaustion that I reel on my feet, I finally give way and sob from the heart like a child: I sit in a corner against the wall and weep, the tears running from my eyes without stop. I weep and weep while the throbbing comes and goes according to its own cycles. In this position sleep bursts upon me like a thunder-bolt. I am amazed to come to myself in the thin grey light of day, slumped in a corner, with not the faintest sense that time has passed. Though the throbbing is still there I find I can endure it if I remain still. Indeed, it has lost its strangeness. Soon, perhaps, it will be as much part of me as breathing.

So I lie quietly against the wall, folding my sore hand under my armpit for comfort, and fall into a second sleep, into a confusion of images among which I search out one in particular, brushing aside the others that fly at me like leaves. It is of the girl. She is kneeling with her back to me before the snowcastle or sandcastle she has built. She wears a dark blue robe. As I approach I see that she is digging away in the bowels of the castle.

She becomes aware of me and turns. I am mistaken, it is not a castle she has built but a clay oven. Smoke curls up from the vent at the back. She holds out her hands to me offering me something, a shapeless lump which I peer at unwillingly through a mist. Though I shake my head my vision will not clear.

She is wearing a round cap embroidered in gold. Her hair is braided in a heavy plait which lies over her shoulder: there is gold thread worked into the braid. 'Why are you dressed in your best?' I want to say: 'I have never seen you looking so lovely.' She smiles at me: what beautiful teeth she has, what clear jet-black eyes! Also now I can see that what she is holding out to me is a loaf of bread, still hot, with a coarse steaming broken crust. A surge of gratitude sweeps through me. 'Where did a child like you learn to bake so well in the desert?' I want to say. I open my arms to embrace her, and come to myself with tears stinging the wound on my cheek. Though I scrabble back at once into the burrow of sleep I cannot re-enter the dream or taste the bread that has made my saliva run.

Colonel Joll sits behind the desk in my office. There are no books or files; the room is starkly empty save for a vase of fresh flowers.

The handsome warrant officer whose name I do not know lifts the cedarwood chest on to the desk and steps back.

Looking down to refer to his papers, the Colonel speaks. 'Among the items found in your apartment was this wooden chest. I would like you to consider it. Its contents are unusual. It contains approximately three hundred slips of white poplar-wood, each about eight inches by two inches, many of them wound about with lengths of string. The wood is dry and brittle. Some of the string is new, some so old that it has perished.

'If one loosens the string one finds that the slip splits open revealing two flat inner surfaces. These surfaces are written on in an unfamiliar script.

'I think you will concur with this description.'

I stare into the black lenses. He goes on.

'A reasonable inference is that the wooden slips contain

messages passed between yourself and other parties, we do not know when. It remains for you to explain what the messages say and who the other parties were.'

He takes a slip from the chest and flicks it across the polished surface of the desk towards me.

I look at the lines of characters written by a stranger long since dead. I do not even know whether to read from right to left or from left to right. In the long evenings I spent poring over my collection I isolated over four hundred different characters in the script, perhaps as many as four hundred and fifty. I have no idea what they stand for. Does each stand for a single thing, a circle for the sun, a triangle for a woman, a wave for a lake; or does a circle merely stand for 'circle', a triangle for 'triangle', a wave for 'wave'? Does each sign represent a different state of the tongue, the lips, the throat, the lungs, as they combine in the uttering of some multifarious unimaginable extinct barbarian language? Or are my four hundred characters nothing but scribal embellishments of an underlying repertory of twenty or thirty whose primitive forms I am too stupid to see?

'He sends greetings to his daughter,' I say. I hear with surprise the thick nasal voice that is now mine. My finger runs along the line of characters from right to left. 'Whom he says he has not seen for a long time. He hopes she is happy and thriving. He hopes the lambing season has been good. He has a gift for her, he says, which he will keep till he sees her again. He sends his love. It is not easy to read his signature. It could be simply "Your father" or it could be something else, a name.'

I reach over into the chest and pick out a second slip. The warrant officer, who sits behind Joll with a little notebook open on his knee, stares hard at me, his pencil poised above the paper.

'This one reads as follows,' I say: ' "I am sorry I must send bad news. The soldiers came and took your brother away. I have been to the fort every day to plead for his return. I sit in the dust with my head bare. Yesterday for the first time they sent a man to speak to me. He says your brother is no longer here. He says he has been sent away. 'Where?' I asked, but he would not say. Do not tell your mother, but join me in praying for his safety."

'And now let us see what this next one says.' The pencil is still poised, he has not written anything, he has not stirred. ' "We went to fetch your brother yesterday. They showed us into a room where he lay on a table sewn up in a sheet." ' Slowly Joll leans back in his chair. The warrant officer closes his notebook and half-rises; but with a gesture Joll restrains him. ' "They wanted me to take him away like that, but I insisted on looking first. 'What if it is the wrong body you are giving me?' I said – 'You have so many bodies here, bodies of brave young men.' So I opened the sheet and saw that it was indeed he. Through each eyelid, I saw, there was a stitch. 'Why have you done that?' I said. 'It is our custom,' he said. I tore the sheet wide open and saw bruises all over his body, and saw that his feet were swollen and broken. 'What happened to him?' I said. 'I do not know,' said the man, 'it is not on the paper; if you have questions you must go to the sergeant, but he is very busy.' We have had to bury your brother here, outside their fort, because he was beginning to stink. Please tell your mother and try to console her." '

'Now let us see what the next one says. See, there is only a single character. It is the barbarian character *war*, but it has other senses too. It can stand for *vengeance*, and, if you turn it upside down like this, it can be made to read *justice*. There is no knowing which sense is intended. That is part of barbarian cunning.

'It is the same with the rest of these slips.' I plunge my good hand into the chest and stir. 'They form an allegory. They can be read in many orders. Further, each single slip can be read in many ways. Together they can be read as a domestic journal, or they can be read as a plan of war, or they can be turned on their sides and read as a history of the last years of the Empire – the old Empire, I mean. There is no agreement among scholars about how to interpret these relics of the ancient barbarians. Allegorical sets like this one can be found buried all over the desert. I found this one not three miles from here in the ruins of a public building. Graveyards are another good place to look in, through it is not always easy to tell where barbarian burial sites lie. It is recommended that you simply dig at random: perhaps at the very spot where you stand you will come upon scraps, shards, reminders of the dead. Also the air: the air is full of sighs and cries. These are never lost: if you listen carefully, with a sympathetic ear, you can hear them echoing forever within the second sphere. The night is best: sometimes when you have difficulty in falling asleep it is because your ears have been reached by the cries of the dead which, like their writings, are open to many interpretations.

'Thank you. I have finished translating.'

I have not failed to keep an eye on Joll through all this. He has not stirred again, save to lay a hand on his subordinate's sleeve at the moment when I referred to the Empire and he rose, ready to strike me.

If he comes near me I will hit him with all the strength in my body. I will not disappear into the earth without leaving my mark on them.

The Colonel speaks. 'You have no idea how tiresome your behaviour is. You are the one and only official we have had to work with on the frontier who has not given us his fullest co-operation. Candidly, I must tell you I am not interested in these sticks.' He waves a hand at the slips scattered on the desk. 'They are very likely gambling-sticks. I know that other tribes on the border gamble with sticks.

'I ask you to consider soberly: what kind of future do you have here? You cannot be allowed to remain in your post. You have utterly disgraced yourself. Even if you are not eventually prosecuted – '

'I am waiting for you to prosecute me!' I shout. 'When are you going to do it? When are you going to bring me to trial? When am I going to have a chance to defend myself?' I am in a fury. None of the speechlessness I felt in front of the crowd afflicts me. If I were to confront these men now, in public, in a fair trial, I would find the words to shame them. It is a matter of health and strength: I feel my hot words swell in my breast.

But they will never bring a man to trial while he is healthy and strong enough to confound them. They will shut me away in the dark till I am a muttering idiot, a ghost of myself; then they will haul me before a closed court and in five minutes dispose of the legalities they find so tiresome.

'For the duration of the emergency, as you know,' says the Colonel, 'the administration of justice is out of the hands of civilians and in the hands of the Bureau.' He sighs. 'Magistrate, you seem to believe that we do not dare to bring you to trial because we fear you are too popular a figure in this town. I do not think you are aware of how much you forfeited by neglecting your duties, shunning your friends, keeping company with low people. There is no one I have spoken to who has not at some time felt insulted by your behaviour.'

'My private life is none of their business!'

'Nevertheless, I may tell you that our decision to relieve you of your duties has been welcomed in most quarters. Personally I have nothing against you. When I arrived back a few days ago, I had decided that all I wanted from you was a clear answer to a simple question, after which you could have returned to your concubines a free man.'

It strikes me suddenly that the insult may not be gratuitous, that perhaps for different reasons these two men might welcome it if I lost my temper. Burning with outrage, tense in every muscle, I guard my silence.

'However, you seem to have a new ambition,' he goes on. 'You seem to want to make a name for yourself as the One Just Man, the man who is prepared to sacrifice his freedom to his principles.

'But let me ask you: do you believe that that is how your fellow-citizens see you after the ridiculous spectacle you created on the square the other day? Believe me, to people in this town you are not the One Just Man, you are simply a clown, a madman. You are dirty, you stink, they can smell you a mile away. You look like an old beggar-man, a refuse-scavenger. They do not want you back in any capacity. You have no future here.

'You want to go down in history as a martyr, I suspect. But who is going to put you in the history books? These border troubles are of no significance. In a while they will pass and the frontier will go to sleep for another twenty years. People are not interested in the history of the back of beyond.'

'There were no border troubles before you came,' I say.

'That is nonsense,' he says. 'You are simply ignorant of the facts. You are living in a world of the past. You think we are dealing with small groups of peaceful nomads. In fact we are dealing with a well organized enemy. If you had travelled with the expeditionary force you would have seen that for yourself.'

'Those pitiable prisoners you brought in – are *they* the enemy I must fear? Is that what you say? *You* are the enemy, Colonel!' I can restrain myself no longer. I pound the desk with my fist. '*You* are the enemy, *you* have made the war, and *you* have given them all the martyrs they need – starting not now but a year ago when you committed your first filthy barbarities here! History will bear me out!'

'Nonsense. There will be no history, the affair is too trivial.' He seems impassive, but I am sure I have shaken him.

'You are an obscene torturer! You deserve to hang!'

'Thus speaks the judge, the One Just Man,' he murmurs.

We stare into each other's eyes.

'Now,' he says, squaring the papers before him: 'I would like a statement on everything that passed between you and the barbarians on your recent and unauthorized visit to them.'

'I refuse.'

'Very well. Our interview is over.' He turns to his subordinate. 'He is your responsibility.' He stands up, walks out. I face the warrant officer.

The wound on my cheek, never washed or dressed, is swollen and inflamed. A crust like a fat caterpillar has formed on it. My left eye is a mere slit, my nose a shapeless throbbing lump. I must breathe through my mouth.

I lie in the reek of old vomit obsessed with the thought of water. I have had nothing to drink for two days.

In my suffering there is nothing ennobling. Little of what I call suffering is even pain. What I am made to undergo is subjection to the most rudimentary needs of my body: to drink, to relieve itself, to find the posture in which it is least sore. When Warrant Officer Mandel and his man first brought me back here and lit the lamp and closed the door, I wondered how much pain a plump comfortable old man would be able to endure in the name of his eccentric notions of how the Empire should conduct itself. But my torturers were not interested in degrees of pain. They were interested only in demonstrating to me what it meant to live in a body, as a body, a body which can entertain notions of justice only as long as it is whole and well, which very soon forgets them when its head is gripped and a pipe is pushed down its gullet and pints of salt water are poured into it till it coughs and retches and flails and voids itself. They did not come to force the story out of me of what I had said to the barbarians and what the barbarians had said to me. So I had no chance to throw the high-sounding words I had ready in their faces. They came to my cell to show me the meaning of humanity, and in the space of an hour they showed me a great deal.

Nor is it a question of who endures longest. I used to think to myself, 'They are sitting in another room discussing me. They are saying to each other, "How much longer before he grovels? In an hour we will go back and see." '

But it is not like that. They have no elaborated system of pain and deprivation to which they subject me. For two days I go without food and water. On the third day I am fed. 'I am sorry,' says the man who brings my food, 'we forgot.' It is not malice that makes them forget. My torturers have their own lives to lead. I am not the centre of their universe. Mandel's underling probably spends his days counting bags in the commissary or patrolling the earthworks, grumbling to himself about the heat. Mandel himself, I am sure, spends more time polishing his straps and buckles than he spends on me. When the mood takes him he comes and gives me a lesson in humanity. How long can I withstand the randomness of their attacks? And what will happen if I succumb, weep, grovel, while yet the attacks go on?

They call me into the yard. I stand before them hiding my nakedness, nursing my sore hand, a tired old bear made tame by too much baiting. 'Run,' Mandel says. I run around the yard under the blazing sun. When I slacken he slaps me on the buttocks with his cane and I trot faster. The soldiers leave their siesta and watch from the shade, the scullery maids hang over the kitchen door, children stare through the bars of the gate. 'I cannot!' I gasp. 'My heart!' I stop, hang my head, clutch my chest. Everyone waits patiently while I recover myself. Then the cane prods me and I shamble on, moving no faster than a man walks.

Or else I do tricks for them. They stretch a rope at knee-height and I jump back and forth over it. They call the cook's little grandson over and give him one end to hold. 'Keep it steady,' they say, 'we don't want him to trip.' The child grips his end of the rope with both hands, concentrating on this important task, waiting for me to jump. I baulk. The point of the cane finds its way between my buttocks and prods. 'Jump,' Mandel murmurs. I run, make a little skip, blunder into the rope, and stand there. I smell of shit. I am not permitted to wash. The flies follow me everywhere, circling around the appetizing sore on my cheek, alighting if I stand still for a moment. The looping movement of my hand before my face to chase them away has become as automatic as the flick of a cow's tail. 'Tell him he must do better next time,' Mandel says to the boy. The boy smiles and looks away. I sit down in the dust to wait for the next trick. 'Do you know how to skip?' he says to the boy. 'Give the rope to the man and ask him to show you how to skip.' I skip.

It cost me agonies of shame the first time I had to come out of my den and stand naked before these idlers or jerk my body about for their amusement. Now I am past shame. My mind is turned wholly to the menace of the moment when my knees turn to water or my heart grips me like a crab and I have to stand still; and each time I discover with surprise that after a little rest, after the application of a little pain, I can be made to move, to jump or skip or crawl or run a little further. Is there a point at which I will lie down and say, 'Kill me – I would rather die than go on'? Sometimes I think I am approaching that point, but I am always mistaken.

There is no consoling grandeur in any of this. When I wake up groaning in the night it is because I am reliving in dreams the pettiest degradations. There is no way of dying allowed me, it seems, except like a dog in a corner.

Then one day they throw open the door and I step out to face not two men but a squad standing to attention. 'Here,' says Mandel, and hands me a woman's calico smock. 'Put it on.'

'Why?'

'Very well, if you want to go naked, go naked.'

I slip the smock over my head. It reaches halfway down my thighs. I catch a glimpse of the two youngest maids ducking back into the kitchen, dissolving in giggles.

My wrists are caught behind my back and tied. 'The time has come, Magistrate,' Mandel whispers in my ear. 'Do your best to behave like a man.' I am sure I can smell liquor on his breath.

They march me out of the yard. Under the mulberry trees, where the earth is purple with the juice of fallen berries, there is a knot of people waiting. Children are scrambling about on the branches. As I approach everyone falls silent.

A soldier tosses up the end of a new white hemp rope; one of the children in the tree catches it, loops it over a branch, and drops it back.

I know this is only a trick, a new way of passing the afternoon

128

for men bored with the old torments. Nevertheless my bowels turn to water. 'Where is the Colonel?' I whisper. No one pays any heed.

'Do you want to say something?' says Mandel. 'Say whatever you wish. We give you this opportunity.'

I look into his clear blue eyes, as clear as if there were crystal lenses slipped over his eyeballs. He looks back at me. I have no idea what he sees. Thinking of him, I have said the words *torture . . . torturer* to myself, but they are strange words, and the more I repeat them the more strange they grow, till they lie like stones on my tongue. Perhaps this man, and the man he brings along to help him with his work, and their Colonel, are torturers, perhaps that is their designation on three cards in a pay-office somewhere in the capital, though it is more likely that the cards call them security officers. But when I look at him I see simply the clear blue eyes, the rather rigid good looks, the teeth slightly too long where the gums are receding. He deals with my soul: every day he folds the flesh aside and exposes my soul to the light; he has probably seen many souls in the course of his working life; but the care of souls seems to have left no more mark on him than the care of hearts leaves on the surgeon.

'I am trying very hard to understand your feelings towards me,' I say. I cannot help mumbling, my voice is unsteady, I am afraid and the sweat is dripping from me. 'Much more than an opportunity to address these people, to whom I have nothing to say, would I appreciate a few words from you. So that I can come to understand why you devote yourself to this work. And can hear what you feel towards me, whom you have hurt a great deal and now seem to be proposing to kill.'

Amazed I stare at this elaborate utterance as it winds its way out of me. Am I mad enough to intend a provocation?

'Do you see this hand?' he says. He holds his hand an inch from my face. 'When I was younger' – he flexes the fingers – 'I used to be able to poke this finger' – he holds up the index finger – 'through a pumpkin-shell.' He puts the tip of his finger against my forehead and presses. I take a step backwards.

They even have a cap ready for me, a salt-bag which they slip over my head and tie around my throat with a string. Through the mesh I watch them bring up the ladder and prop it against the branch. I am guided to it, my foot is set on the lowest rung, the noose is settled under my ear. 'Now climb,' says Mandel.

I turn my head and see two dim figures holding the end of the rope. 'I can't climb with my hands tied,' I say. My heart is hammering. 'Climb,' he says, steadying me by the arm. The rope tightens. 'Keep it tight,' he orders.

I climb, he climbs behind me, guiding me. I count ten rungs. Leaves brush against me. I stop. He grips my arm tighter. 'Do you think we are playing?' he says. He talks through clenched teeth in a fury I do not understand. 'Do you think I don't mean what I say?'

My eyes sting with sweat inside the bag. 'No,' I say, 'I do not think you are playing.' As long as the rope remains taut I know they are playing. If the rope goes slack, and I slip, I will die.

'Then what do you want to say to me?'

'I want to say that nothing passed between myself and the barbarians concerning military matters. It was a private affair. I went to return the girl to her family. For no other purpose.'

'Is that all you want to say to me?'

'I want to say that no one deserves to die.' In my absurd frock and bag, with the nausea of cowardice in my mouth, I say: 'I want to live. As every man wants to live. To live and live and live. No matter what.'

'That isn't enough.' He lets my arm go. I teeter on my tenth rung, the rope saving my balance. 'Do you see?' he says. He retreats down the ladder, leaving me alone.

Not sweat but tears.

There is a rustling in the leaves near me. A child's voice: 'Can you see, uncle?'

'No.'

'Hey, monkeys, come down!' calls someone from below.

Through the taut rope I can feel the vibration of their movements in the branches.

So I stand for a long while, balancing carefully on the rung, feeling the comfort of the wood in the curve of my sole, trying not to waver, keeping the tension of the rope as constant as possible.

How long will a crowd of idlers be content to watch a man stand on a ladder? I would stand here till the flesh dropped from my bones, through storm and hail and flood, to live.

But now the rope tightens, I can even hear it rasp as it passes over the bark, till I must stretch to keep it from throttling me.

This is not a contest of patience, then: if the crowd is not satisfied the rules are changed. But of what use is it to blame the crowd? A scapegoat is named, a festival is declared, the laws are suspended: who would not flock to see the entertainment? What is it I object to in these spectacles of abasement and suffering and death that our new regime puts on but their lack of decorum? What will my own administration be remembered for besides moving the shambles from the marketplace to the outskirts of the town twenty years ago in the interests of decency? I try to call out something, a word of blind fear, a shriek, but the rope is now so tight that I am strangled, speechless. The blood hammers in my ears. I feel my toes lose their hold. I am swinging gently in the air, bumping against the ladder, flailing with my feet. The drumbeat in my ears becomes slower and louder till it is all I can hear.

I am standing in front of the old man, screwing up my eyes against the wind, waiting for him to speak. The ancient gun still rests between his horse's ears, but it is not aimed at me. I am aware of the vastness of the sky all around us, and of the desert.

I watch his lips. At any moment now he will speak: I must listen carefully to capture every syllable, so that later, repeating them to myself, poring over them, I can discover the answer to a question which for the moment has flown like a bird from my recollection.

I can see every hair of the horse's mane, every wrinkle of the old man's face, every rock and furrow of the hillside.

The girl, with her black hair braided and hanging over her shoulder in barbarian fashion, sits her horse behind him. Her head is bowed, she too is waiting for him to speak.

I sigh. 'What a pity,' I think. 'It is too late now.'

I am swinging loose. The breeze lifts my smock and plays with my naked body. I am relaxed, floating. In a woman's clothes.

What must be my feet touch the ground, though they are numb to all feeling. I stretch myself out carefully, at full length, light as a leaf. Whatever it is that has held my head so tightly slackens its grip. From inside me comes a ponderous grating. I breathe. All is well.

Then the hood comes off, the sun dazzles my eyes, I am hauled to my feet, everything swims before me, I go blank.

The word *flying* whispers itself somewhere at the edge of my consciousness. Yes, it is true, I have been flying.

I am looking into the blue eyes of Mandel. His lips move but I hear no words. I shake my head, and having once started find that I cannot stop.

'I was saying,' he says, '*now we will show you another form of flying.*'

'He can't hear you,' someone says. 'He can hear,' says Mandel. He slips the noose from my neck and knots it around the cord that binds my wrists. 'Pull him up.'

If I can hold my arms stiff, if I am acrobat enough to swing a foot up and hook it around the rope, I will be able to hang upside down and not be hurt: that is my last thought before they begin to hoist me. But I am as weak as a baby, my arms come up behind my back, and as my feet leave the ground I feel a terrible tearing in my shoulders as though whole sheets of muscle are giving way. From my throat comes the first mournful dry bellow, like the pouring of gravel. Two little boys drop out of the tree and, hand in hand, not looking back, trot off. I bellow again and again, there is nothing I can do to stop it, the noise comes out of a body that knows itself damaged perhaps beyond repair and roars its fright. Even if all the children of the town should hear me I cannot stop myself: let us only pray that they do not imitate their elders' games, or tomorrow there will be a plague of little bodies dangling from the trees. Someone gives me a push and I begin to float back and forth in an arc a foot above the ground like a great old moth with its wings pinched together, roaring, shouting. 'He is calling his barbarian friends,' someone observes. 'That is barbarian language you hear.' There is laughter.

V

The barbarians come out at night. Before darkness falls the last goat must be brought in, the gates barred, a watch set in every lookout to call the hours. All night, it is said, the barbarians prowl about bent on murder and rapine. Children in their dreams see the shutters part and fierce barbarian faces leer through. 'The barbarians are here!' the children scream, and cannot be comforted. Clothing disappears from washing-lines, food from larders, however tightly locked. The barbarians have dug a tunnel under the walls, people say; they come and go as they please, take what they like; no one is safe any longer. The farmers still till the fields, but they go out in bands, never singly. They work without heart: the barbarians are only waiting for the crops to be established, they say, before they flood the fields again.

Why doesn't the army stop the barbarians? people complain. Life on the frontier has become too hard. They talk of returning to the Old Country, but then remember that the roads are no longer safe because of the barbarians. Tea and sugar can no longer be bought over the counter as the shopkeepers hoard their stocks. Those who eat well eat behind closed doors, fearful of awaking their neighbour's envy.

Three weeks ago a little girl was raped. Her friends, playing in the irrigation ditches, did not miss her till she came back to them bleeding, speechless. For days she lay in her parents' home staring at the ceiling. Nothing would induce her to tell her story. When the lamp was put out she would begin to whimper. Her friends claim a barbarian did it. They saw him running away into the reeds. They recognized him as a barbarian by his ugliness. Now all children are forbidden to play outside the gates, and the farmers carry clubs and spears when they go to the fields.

The higher feeling runs against the barbarians, the tighter I huddle in my corner, hoping I will not be remembered.

It is a long time since the second expeditionary force rode out so bravely with its flags and trumpets and shining armour and prancing steeds to sweep the barbarians from the valley and teach them a lesson they and their children and grandchildren would never forget. Since then there have been no dispatches, no communiqués. The exhilaration of the times when there used to be daily military parades on the square, displays of horsemanship, exhibitions of musketry, has long since dissipated. Instead the air is full of anxious rumours. Some say that the entire thousand-mile frontier has erupted into conflict, that the northern barbarians have joined forces with the western barbarians, that the army of the Empire is too thinly stretched, that one of these days it will be forced to give up the defence of remote outposts like this one to concentrate its resources on the protection of the heartland. Others say that we receive no news of the war only because our soldiers have thrust deep into the enemy's territory and are too busy dealing out heavy blows to send dispatches. Soon, they say, when we least expect it, our men will come marching back weary but victorious, and we shall have peace in our time.

Among the small garrison that has been left behind there is more drunkenness than I have ever known before, more arrogance towards the townspeople. There have been incidents in which soldiers have gone into shops, taken what they wanted, and left without paying. Of what use is it for the shopkeeper to raise the alarm when the criminals and the civil guard are the same people? The shopkeepers complain to Mandel, who is in charge under the emergency powers while Joll is away with the army. Mandel makes promises but does not act. Why should he? All that matters to him is that he should remain popular with his men. Despite the parade of vigilance on the ramparts and the weekly sweep along the lakeshore (for lurking barbarians, though none has ever been caught), discipline is lax.

Meanwhile I, the old clown who lost his last vestige of authority the day he spent hanging from a tree in a woman's underclothes shouting for help, the filthy creature who for a week licked his food off the flagstones like a dog because he had lost the use of his hands, am no longer locked up. I sleep in a corner of the barracks yard; I creep around in my filthy smock; when a fist is raised against me I cower. I live like a starved beast at the back door, kept alive perhaps only as evidence of the animal that skulks within every barbarian-lover. I know I am not safe. Sometimes I can feel the weight of a resentful gaze resting upon me; I do not look up; I know that for some the attraction must be strong to clear the yard by putting a bullet through my skull from an upstairs window.

There has been a drift of refugees to the town, fisherfolk from the tiny settlements dotted along the river and the northern lakeshore, speaking a language no one understands, carrying their households on their backs, with their gaunt dogs and rickety children trailing behind them. People crowded around them when they first came. 'Was it the barbarians who chased you out?' they asked, making fierce faces, stretching imaginary bows. No one asked about the imperial soldiery or the brushfires they set.

There was sympathy for these savages at first, and people brought them food and old clothing, until they began to put up their thatched shelters against the wall on the side of the square near the walnut trees, and their children grew bold enough to sneak into kitchens and steal, and one night a pack of their dogs broke into the sheepfold and tore out the throats of a dozen ewes. Feelings then turned against them. The soldiers took action, shooting their dogs on sight and, one morning when the men were still down at the lake, tearing down the entire row of shelters. For days the fisherfolk hid out in the reeds. Then one by one their little thatched huts began to reappear, this time outside the town under the north wall. Their huts were allowed to stand, but the sentries at the gate received orders to deny them entry. Now that rule has been relaxed, and they can be seen hawking strings of fish from door to door in the mornings. They have no experience of money, they are cheated outrageously, they will part with anything for a thimbleful of rum.

They are a bony, pigeon-chested people. Their women seem always to be pregnant; their children are stunted; in a few of the young girls there are traces of a fragile, liquid-eyed beauty; for the rest I see only ignorance, cunning, slovenliness. Yet what do they see in me, if they ever see me? A beast that stares out from behind a gate: the filthy underside of this beautiful oasis where they have found a precarious safety.

One day a shadow falls across me where I doze in the yard, a foot prods me, and I look up into Mandel's blue eyes.

'Are we feeding you well?' he says. 'Are you growing fat again?'

I nod, sitting at his feet.

'Because we can't go on feeding you forever.'

There is a long pause while we examine each other.

'When are you going to begin working for your keep?'

'I am a prisoner awaiting trial. Prisoners awaiting trial are not required to work for their keep. That is the law. They are maintained out of the public coffer.'

'But you are not a prisoner. You are free to go as you please.' He waits for me to take the ponderously offered bait. I say nothing. He goes on: 'How can you be a prisoner when we have no record of you? Do you think we don't keep records? We have no record of you. So you must be a free man.'

I rise and follow him across the yard to the gate. The guard hands him the key and he unlocks it. 'You see? The gate is open.'

I hesitate before I pass through. There is something I would like to know. I look into Mandel's face, at the clear eyes, windows of his soul, at the mouth from which his spirit utters itself. 'Have you a minute to spare?' I say. We stand in the gateway, with the guard in the background pretending not to hear. I say: 'I am not a young man any more, and whatever future I had in this place is in ruins.' I gesture around the square,

137

at the dust that scuds before the hot late summer wind, bringer of blights and plagues. 'Also I have already died one death, on that tree, only you decided to save me. So there is something I would like to know before I go. If it is not too late, with the barbarian at the gate.' I feel the tiniest smile of mockery brush my lips, I cannot help it. I glance up at the empty sky. 'Forgive me if the question seems impudent, but I would like to ask: How do you find it possible to eat afterwards, after you have been . . . working with people? That is a question I have always asked myself about executioners and other such people. Wait! Listen to me a moment longer, I am sincere, it has cost me a great deal to come out with this, since I am terrified of you, I need not tell you that, I am sure you are aware of it. Do you find it easy to take food afterwards? I have imagined that one would want to wash one's hands. But no ordinary washing would be enough, one would require priestly intervention, a ceremonial of cleansing, don't you think? Some kind of purging of one's soul too – that is how I have imagined it. Otherwise how would it be possible to return to everyday life – to sit down at table, for instance, and break bread with one's family or one's comrades?'

He turns away, but with a slow claw-like hand I manage to catch his arm. 'No, listen!' I say. 'Do not misunderstand me, I am not blaming you or accusing you, I am long past that. Remember, I too have devoted a life to the law, I know its processes, I know that the workings of justice are often obscure. I am only trying to understand. I am trying to understand the zone in which you live. I am trying to imagine how you breathe and eat and live from day to day. But I cannot! That is what troubles me! If I were he, I say to myself, my hands would feel so dirty that it would choke me – '

He wrenches himself free and hits me so hard in the chest that I gasp and stumble backwards. 'You bastard!' he shouts. 'You fucking old lunatic! Get out! Go and die somewhere!'

'When are you going to put me on trial?' I shout at his retreating back. He pays no heed.

*

There is nowhere to hide. And why should I? From dawn to dusk I am on view on the square, roaming around the stalls or sitting in the shade of the trees. And gradually, as word gets around that the old Magistrate has taken his knocks and come through, people cease to fall silent or turn their backs when I come near. I discover that I am not without friends, particularly among women, who can barely conceal their eagerness to hear my side of the story. Roaming the streets, I pass the quartermaster's plump wife hanging out the washing. We greet. 'And how are you, sir?' she says. 'We heard that you had such a hard time.' Her eyes glitter, avid though cautious. 'Won't you come in and have a cup of tea?' So we sit together at the kitchen table, and she sends the children to play outside, and while I drink tea and munch steadily at a plate of the delicious oatmeal biscuits she bakes, she plays out the first moves in this roundabout game of question and answer: 'You were gone so long, we wondered if you would ever be coming back . . . And then all the trouble you had! How things have changed! There was none of this commotion when you were in charge. All these strangers from the capital, upsetting things!' I take my cue, sigh: 'Yes, they don't understand how we go about things in the provinces, do they. All this trouble over a girl . . .' I gobble another biscuit. A fool in love is laughed at but in the end always forgiven. 'To me it was simply a matter of common sense to take her back to her family, but how could one make them understand that?' I ramble on; she listens to these half-truths, nodding, watching me like a hawk; we pretend that the voice she hears is not the voice of the man who swung from the tree shouting for mercy loud enough to waken the dead. ' . . . Anyhow, let us hope it is all over. I still have pains' – I touch my shoulder – 'one's body heals so slowly as one gets older . . .'

So I sing for my keep. And if I am still hungry in the evening, if I wait at the barracks gate for the whistle that calls the dogs and slip in quietly enough, I can usually wheedle out of the maids the leftovers from the soldiers' supper, a bowl of cold beans or the rich scrapings of the soup-pot or half a loaf of bread.

Or in the mornings I can saunter over to the inn and, leaning over the flap of the kitchen door, breathe in all the good smells, marjoram and yeast and crisp chopped onions and smoky mutton-fat. Mai the cook greases the baking-pans: I watch her deft fingers dip into the pot of lard and coat the pan in three swift circles. I think of her pastries, the renowned ham and spinach and cheese pie she makes, and feel the saliva spurt in my mouth.

'So many people have left,' she says, turning to the great ball of dough, 'I can't even begin to tell you. A sizable party left only a few days ago. One of the girls from here – the little one with the long straight hair, you may remember her – she was one of them, she left with her fellow.' Her voice is flat as she imparts the information to me, and I am grateful for her considerateness. 'Of course it makes sense,' she continues, 'if you want to leave you must leave now, it's a long road, dangerous too, and the nights are getting colder.' She talks about the weather, about the past summer and signs of approaching winter, as though where I had been, in my cell not three hundred paces from where we stand, I had been sealed off from hot and cold, dry and wet. To her, I realize, I disappeared and then reappeared, and in between was not part of the world.

I have been listening and nodding and dreaming while she talks. Now I speak. 'You know,' I say, 'when I was in prison – in the barracks, not in the new prison, in a little room they locked me into – I was so hungry that I did not give a thought to women, only to food. I lived from one mealtime to the next. There was never enough for me. I bolted my food like a dog and wanted more. Also there was a great deal of pain, at different times: my hand, my arms, as well as this' – I touch the thickened nose, the ugly scar under my eye by which, I am beginning to learn, people are surreptitiously fascinated. 'When I dreamed of a woman I dreamed of someone who would come in the night and take the pain away. A child's dream. What I did not know was how longing could store itself away in the hollows of one's bones and then one day without warning flood out. What you said a moment ago, for instance – the girl you mentioned – I was very fond of her, I think you know that, though delicacy prevented you . . . When you said she was gone, I confess, it was as if something had struck me here, in the breast. A blow.'

Her hands move deftly, pressing circles out of the sheet of dough with the rim of a bowl, catching up the scraps, rolling them together. She avoids my eyes.

'I went upstairs to her room last night, but the door was locked. I shrugged it off. She has a lot of friends, I never thought I was the only one . . . But what did I want? Somewhere to sleep, certainly; but more too. Why pretend? We all know, what old men seek is to recover their youth in the arms of young women.' She pounds the dough, kneads it, rolls it out: a young woman herself with children of her own, living with an exacting mother: what appeal am I making to her as I ramble on about pain, loneliness? Bemused I listen to the discourse that emerges from me. 'Let everything be said!' I told myself when I first faced up to my tormentors. 'Why clamp your lips stupidly together? You have no secrets. Let them know they are working on flesh and blood! Declare your terror, scream when the pain comes! They thrive on stubborn silence: it confirms to them that every soul is a lock they must patiently pick. Bare yourself! Open your heart!' So I shouted and screamed and said whatever came into my head. Insidious rationale! For now what I hear when I loosen my tongue and let it sail free is the subtle whining of a beggar. 'Do you know where I slept last night?' I hear myself saying. 'Do you know that little lean-to at the back of the granary? . . .'

But above all it is food that I crave, and more intensely with every passing week. I want to be fat again. There is a hunger upon me day and night. I wake up with my stomach yawning, I cannot wait to be on my rounds, loitering at the barracks gate to sniff the bland watery aroma of oatmeal and wait for the burnt scrapings; cajoling children to throw me down mulberries from the trees; stretching over a garden fence to steal a peach or two; passing from door to door, a man down on his luck, the victim of an infatuation, but cured now, ready with a smile to take what is offered, a slice of bread and jam, a cup of tea, in the middle of the day perhaps a bowl of stew or a plate of onions and beans, and always fruit, apricots, peaches, pomegranates, the wealth of a bounteous summer. I eat like a beggar, gobbling down my food with such appetite, wiping my plate so clean that it does the heart good to see it. No wonder I am day by day creeping back into the good books of my countrymen.

And how I can flatter, how I can woo! More than once have I had a tasty snack prepared especially for me: a mutton chop fried with peppers and chives, or a slice of ham and tomato on bread with a wedge of goats' milk cheese. If I can carry water or firewood in return, I do so gladly, as a token, though I am not as strong as I used to be. And if for the time being I have exhausted my sources in the town – for I must be careful not to become a burden on my benefactors – I can always stroll down to the fisherfolk's camp and help them clean fish. I have learned a few words of their language, I am received without suspicion, they understand what it is to be a beggar, they share their food with me.

I want to be fat again, fatter than ever before. I want a belly that gurgles with contentment when I fold my palms over it, I want to feel my chin sink into the cushion of my throat and my breasts wobble as I walk. I want a life of simple satisfactions. I want (vain hope!) never to know hunger again.

Nearly three months since it departed, and still there is no news of the expeditionary force. Instead, terrible rumours everywhere: that the force has been lured into the desert and wiped out; that unknown to us it has been recalled to defend the homeland, leaving the frontier towns for the barbarians to pick like fruit whenever they choose to. Every week there is a convoy of the prudent leaving town, going east, ten or twelve families travelling together 'to visit relatives', as the euphemism has it, 'till things settle down again'. They leave, leading pack-trains, pushing handcarts, carrying packs on their backs, their very children laden like beasts. I have even seen a long low four-wheeled cart drawn by sheep. Pack-animals can no longer be bought. Those who depart are the sensible ones, the husbands and wives who lie awake in bed whispering, making plans, cutting losses. They leave their comfortable homes behind, locking them 'till we return', taking the keys as a memento. By the next day gangs of soldiers have broken in, looted the houses, smashed the furniture, fouled the floors. Resentment builds up against those who are seen to be making preparations to go. They are insulted in public, assaulted or robbed with impunity. Now there are families that simply disappear in the dead of night, bribing the guards to open the gates for them, taking the east road and waiting at the first or second stopping-place till the party that accumulates is large enough to travel safely.

The soldiery tyrannizes the town. They have held a torchlight meeting on the square to denounce 'cowards and traitors' and to affirm collective allegiance to the Empire. *WE STAY* has become the slogan of the faithful: the words are to be seen daubed on walls everywhere. I stood in the dark on the edge of the huge crowd that night (no one was brave enough to stay at home) listening to these words chanted ponderously, menacingly from thousands of throats. A shiver ran down my back. After the meeting the soldiers led a procession through the streets. Doors were kicked in, windows broken, a house set on fire. Till late at night there was drinking and carousing on the square. I looked out for Mandel but did not see him. It may be that he has lost control of the garrison, if indeed the soldiers were ever prepared to take orders from a policeman.

When they were first quartered on the town these soldiers, strangers to our ways, conscripts from all over the Empire, were welcomed coolly. 'We don't need them here,' people said, 'the sooner they go out and fight the barbarians the better.' They were denied credit in the shops, mothers locked their daughters away from them. But after the barbarians made their appearance on our doorstep that attitude changed. Now that they seem to be all that stands between us and destruction, these foreign soldiers are anxiously courted. A committee of citizens makes a weekly levy to hold a feast for them, roasting whole sheep on spits, laying out gallons of rum. The girls of the town are theirs for the taking. They are welcome to whatever they want as long as they will stay and guard our lives. And the more they are fawned on, the more their arrogance grows. We know we cannot rely on them. With the granary nearly empty and the main force vanished like smoke, what is there to hold them once the feasting stops? All we can hope for is that they will be deterred from deserting us by the rigours of winter travel.

For premonitions of winter are everywhere. In the early hours of the morning a chilly breeze rises in the north: the shutters creak, sleepers huddle closer, the sentries wrap their cloaks tight, turn their backs. Some nights I wake up shivering on my bed of sacks and cannot get to sleep again. When the sun comes up it seems farther away each day; the earth grows cold even before sunset. I think of the little convoys of travellers strung out along hundreds of miles of road, heading for a motherland most have never seen, pushing their handcarts, goading their horses, carrying their children, nursing their provisions, day by day abandoning at the roadside tools, kitchenware, portraits, clocks, toys, everything they believed they might rescue from the ruin of their estates before they realized that at most they might hope to escape with their lives. In a week or two the weather will be too treacherous for any but the hardiest to set out. The bleak north wind will be howling all day, withering life on the stalk, carrying a sea of dust across the wide plateau, bringing sudden flurries of hail and snow. I cannot imagine myself, with my tattered clothes and cast-off sandals, stick in hand, pack on back, surviving that long march. My heart would not be in it. What life can I hope for away from this oasis? The life of an indigent bookkeeper in the capital, coming back every evening after dusk to a rented room in a back street, with my teeth slowly falling out and the landlady sniffing at the door? If I were to join the exodus it would be as one of those unobtrusive old folk who one day slip away from the line of march, settle down in the lee of a rock, and wait for the last great cold to begin creeping up their legs.

I wander down the wide road down to the lakeside. The horizon ahead is already grey, merging into the grey water of the lake. Behind me the sun is setting in streaks of gold and crimson. From the ditches comes the first cricketsong. This is a world I know and love and do not want to leave. I have walked this road by night since my youth and come to no harm. How can I believe that the night is full of the flitting shadows of barbarians? If there were strangers here I would feel it in my bones. The barbarians have withdrawn with their flocks into the deepest mountain valleys, waiting for the soldiers to grow tired and go away. When that happens the barbarians will come out again. They will graze their sheep and leave us alone, we will plant our fields and leave them alone, and in a few years the frontier will be restored to peace.

I pass the ruined fields, cleared by now and ploughed afresh, cross the irrigation ditches and the shore-wall. The ground beneath my soles grows soft; soon I am walking on soggy marshgrass, pushing my way through reedbrakes, striding ankle-deep in water in the last violet light of dusk. Frogs plop into the water before me; nearby I hear a faint rustle of feathers as a marshbird crouches ready to fly.

I wade deeper, parting the reeds with my hands, feeling the cool slime between my toes; the water, holding the warmth of the sun longer than the air, resists, then gives way, before each stride. In the early hours of the morning the fishermen pole their flat-bottomed boats out across this calm surface and cast their nets. What a peaceful way to make a living! Perhaps I should leave off my beggar's trade and join them in their camp outside the wall, build myself a hut of mud and reeds, marry one of their pretty daughters, feast when the catch is plentiful, tighten my belt when it is not.

Calf-deep in the soothing water I indulge myself in this wistful vision. I am not unaware of what such daydreams signify, dreams of becoming an unthinking savage, of taking the cold road back to the capital, of groping my way out to the ruins in the desert, of returning to the confinement of my cell, of seeking out the barbarians and offering myself to them to use as they wish. Without exception they are dreams of ends: dreams not of how to live but of how to die. And everyone, I know, in that walled town sinking now into darkness (I hear the two thin trumpet calls that announce the closing of the gates) is similarly preoccupied. Everyone but the children! The children never doubt that the great old trees in whose shade they play will stand forever, that one day they will grow to be strong like their fathers, fertile like their mothers, that they will live and prosper and raise their own children and grow old in the place where they were born. What has made it impossible for us to live in time like fish in water, like birds in air, like children? It is the fault of Empire! Empire has created the time of history. Empire has located its existence not in the smooth recurrent spinning time of the cycle of the seasons but in the jagged time of rise and fall, of beginning and end, of catastrophe. Empire dooms itself to live in history and plot against history. One thought alone preoccupies the submerged mind of Empire: how not to end, how not to die, how to prolong its era. By day it pursues its enemies. It is cunning and ruthless, it sends its bloodhounds everywhere. By night it feeds on images of disaster: the sack of cities, the rape of populations, pyramids of bones, acres of desolation. A mad vision yet a virulent one: I, wading in the ooze, am no less infected with it than the faithful Colonel Joll as he tracks the enemies of Empire through the boundless desert, sword unsheathed to cut down barbarian after barbarian until at last he finds and slays the one whose destiny it should be (or if not his then his son's or unborn grandson's) to climb the bronze gateway to the Summer Palace and topple the globe surmounted by the tiger rampant that symbolizes eternal dominion, while his comrades below cheer and fire their muskets in the air.

There is no moon. In darkness I grope my way back to dry land and on a bed of grass, wrapped in my cloak, fall asleep. I wake up stiff and cold from a flurry of confused dreams. The red star has barely moved in the sky.

As I pass along the road to the fishermen's camp a dog starts to bark; in a moment it is joined by another, and the night bursts out in a clamour of barking, shouts of alarm, screams. Dismayed, I shout out at the top of my voice, 'It is nothing!' but I am not heard. I stand helpless in the middle of the road. Someone runs past me down towards the lake; then another body cannons into me, a woman, I know at once, who gasps in terror in my arms before she breaks free and is gone. There are dogs, too, snarling about me: I whirl and cry out as one snaps at my legs, tears my skin, retreats. The frenzied yapping is all round me. From behind the walls the dogs of the town bay their response. I crouch and circle, tensed for the next attack. The brassy wail of trumpets cuts through the air. The dogs bark louder than ever. Slowly I shuffle towards the camp, till one of the huts suddenly looms against the sky. I push aside the mat that hangs over the doorway and pass into the sweaty warmth where until a few minutes ago people slept.

The clamour outside dies down, but no one returns. The air is stale, drowsy. I would like to sleep, yet I am disturbed by the resonance of that soft impact on me in the road. Like a bruise my flesh retains the imprint of the body that for a few seconds rested against me. I fear what I am capable of: of coming back tomorrow in daylight still aching with the memory and asking questions until I discover who it was who ran into me in the dark, so as to build upon her, child or woman, an even more ridiculous erotic adventure. There is no limit to the foolishness of men of my age. Our only excuse is that we leave no mark of our own on the girls who pass through our hands: our convoluted desires, our ritualized lovemaking, our elephantine ecstasies are soon forgotten, they shrug off our clumsy dance as they drive straight as arrows into the arms of the men whose children they will bear, the young and vigorous and direct. Our loving leaves no mark. Whom will that other girl with the blind face remember: me with my silk robe and my dim lights and my perfumes and oils and my unhappy pleasures, or that other cold man with the mask over his eyes who gave the orders and pondered the sounds of her intimate pain? Whose was the last face she saw plainly on this earth but the face behind the glowing iron? Though I cringe with shame, even here and now, I must ask myself whether, when I lay head to foot with her, fondling and kissing those broken ankles, I was not in my heart of hearts regretting that I could not engrave myself on her as deeply. However kindly she may be treated by her own people, she will never be courted and married in the normal way: she is marked for life as the property of a stranger, and no one will approach her save in the spirit of lugubrious sensual pity that she detected and rejected in me. No wonder she fell asleep so often, no wonder she was happier peeling vegetables than in my bed! From the moment my steps paused and I stood before her at the barracks gate she must have felt a miasma of deceit closing about her: envy, pity, cruelty all masquerading as desire. And in my lovemaking not impulse but the laborious denial of impulse! I remember her sober smile. From the very first she knew me for a false seducer. She listened to me, then she listened to her heart, and rightly she acted in accord with her heart. If only she had found the words to tell me! 'That is not how you do it,' she should have said, stopping me in the act. 'If you want to learn how to do it, ask your friend with the black eyes.' Then she should have continued, so as not to leave me without hope: 'But if you want to love me you will have to turn your back on him and learn your lesson elsewhere.' If she had told me then, if I had understood her, if I had been in a position to understand her, if I had believed her, if I had been in a position to believe her, I might have saved myself from a year of confused and futile gestures of expiation.

For I was not, as I liked to think, the indulgent pleasure-loving opposite of the cold rigid Colonel. I was the lie that Empire tells itself when times are easy, he the truth that Empire tells when harsh winds blow. Two sides of Imperial rule, no more, no less. But I temporized, I looked around this obscure frontier, this little backwater with its dusty summers and its cartloads of apricots and its long siestas and its shiftless garrison and the waterbirds flying in and flying out year after year to and from the dazzling waveless sheet of the lake, and I said to myself, 'Be patient, one of these days he will go away, one of these days quiet will return: then our siestas will grow longer and our swords rustier, the watchman will sneak down from his tower to spend the night with his wife, the mortar will crumble till lizards nest between the bricks and owls fly out of the belfry, and the line that marks the frontier on the maps of Empire will grow hazy and obscure till we are blessedly forgotten.' Thus I seduced myself, taking one of the many wrong turnings I have taken on a road that looks true but has delivered me into the heart of a labyrinth.

In the dream I am advancing towards her over the snow-covered square. At first I walk. Then as the wind gathers force I begin to be driven forward in a cloud of whirling snow, with arms extended on either side and the wind catching my cloak like a boatsail. Gathering speed, my feet skimming over the ground, I swoop down upon the solitary figure at the centre of the square. 'She will not turn and see me in time!' I think. I open my mouth to cry out a warning. A thin wail comes to my ears, whipped away by the wind, borne up into the sky like a scrap of paper. I am almost upon her, I am already tensing myself for the impact, when she turns and sees me. For an instant I have a vision of her face, the face of a child, glowing, healthy, smiling on me without alarm, before we collide. Her head strikes me in the belly; then I am gone, carried by the wind. The bump is as faint as the stroke of a moth. I am flooded with relief. 'Then I need not have been anxious after all!' I think. I try to look back, but all is lost from sight in the whiteness of the snow.

My mouth is covered in wet kisses. I spit, shake my head, open my eyes. The dog that has been licking my face backs off wagging its tail. Light seeps through the doorway of the hut. I crawl out into the dawn. Sky and water are tinged with the same rosiness. The lake, where I have grown used to seeing every morning the blunt-prowed fishing-boats, is empty. The camp where I stand is empty too.

I wrap myself tighter in my cloak and walk up the road past the main gate, which is still closed, as far as the north-west watchtower, which does not appear to be manned; then back down the road and, cutting across the fields, over the earthwall towards the lakeside.

A hare starts at my feet and dashes away in a zigzag. I keep track of it until it has circled back and is lost behind the ripe wheat in the far fields.

A little boy stands in the middle of the path fifty yards from me, peeing. He watches the arc of his urine, watching me too out of the corner of his eye, curving his back to make the last spurt go further. Then with his golden trail still hanging in the air he is suddenly gone, snatched away by a dark arm from the reeds.

I stand on the spot where he stood. There is nothing to be seen but tossing reed-crests through which flickers the dazzling half-globe of the sun.

'You can come out,' I say, barely raising my voice. 'There is nothing to be afraid of.' The finches, I notice, are avoiding this patch of reeds. I have no doubt that thirty pairs of ears hear me.

I turn back to the town.

The gates are open. Soldiers, heavily armed, poke around among the huts of the fisherfolk. The dog that awoke me trots with them from hut to hut, tail high, tongue lolling, ears alert.

One of the soldiers heaves at the rack where the gutted and salted fish hang to dry. It comes creaking down.

'Don't do that!' I call, hurrying my steps. Some of these men I recognize from the long days of torment in the barracks yard. 'Don't do it, it wasn't their fault!'

With deliberate nonchalance the same soldier now strolls over to the largest of the huts, braces himself against two of the projecting roof-struts, and tries to lift the thatched roof off. Though he strains he cannot do it. I have watched these fragile-seeming huts being built. They are built to withstand the tugging of winds in which no bird can fly. The roof frame is lashed to the uprights with thongs that pass through wedge-shaped notches. One cannot lift it without cutting the thongs.

I plead with the man. 'Let me tell you what happened last night. I was walking past in the dark and the dogs began to bark. The people here were frightened, they lost their heads, you know how they are. They probably thought the barbarians had come. They ran away down to the lake. They are hiding in the reeds – I saw them a short while ago. You can't punish them for such a ridiculous incident.'

He ignores me. A comrade helps him to clamber on to the roof. Balancing on two struts, he begins to stamp holes in the roof with the heel of his boot. I hear the thuds inside as the grass and clay plastering falls.

'Stop it!' I shout. The blood pounds in my temples. 'What have they done to harm you?' I grab at his ankle but he is too far away. I could tear out his throat in this mood.

Someone thrusts himself before me: the friend who helped him up. 'Why don't you fuck off,' he murmurs. 'Why don't you just fuck off. Why don't you go and die somewhere.'

Under the thatch and clay I hear the roof-strut snap cleanly. The man on the roof throws out his hands and plunges through. One moment he is there, his eyes wide with surprise, the next moment there is only a puff of dust hanging in the air.

The mat over the doorway is pushed aside and he staggers out clutching his hands together, covered from head to toe in ochre dust. 'Shit!' he says. 'Shit, shit, shit, shit, shit!' His friends howl with laughter. 'It's not funny!' he shouts. 'I've hurt my fucking thumb!' He squeezes his hand between his knees. 'It's fucking sore!' He swings a kick at the wall of the hut and again I hear plaster fall inside. 'Fucking savages!' he says. 'We should have lined them up against a wall and shot them long ago – with their friends!'

Looking past me, looking through me, declining in every way to see me, he swaggers off. As he passes the last hut he rips off the mat over the doorway. The strings of beads with which it is decorated, red and black berries, dried melon-seeds, break and cascade everywhere. I stand in the road waiting for the quivering of rage in me to subside. I think of a young peasant who was once brought before me in the days when I had jurisdiction over the garrison. He had been committed to the army for three years by a magistrate in a far-off town for stealing chickens. After a month here he tried to desert. He was caught and brought before me. He wanted to see his mother and his sisters again, he said. 'We cannot just do as we wish,' I lectured him. 'We are all subject to the law, which is greater than any of us. The magistrate who sent you here, I myself, you – we are all subject to the law.' He looked at me with dull eyes, waiting to hear the punishment, his two stolid escorts behind him, his hands manacled behind his back. 'You feel that it is unjust, I know, that you should be punished for having the feelings of a good son. You think you know what is just and what is not. I understand. We all think we know.' I had no doubt, myself, then, that at each moment each one of us, man, woman, child, perhaps even the poor old horse turning the mill-wheel, knew what was just: all creatures come into the world bringing with them the memory of justice. 'But we live in a world of laws,' I said to my poor prisoner, 'a world of the second-best. There is nothing we can do about that. We are fallen creatures. All we can do is to uphold the laws, all of us, without allowing the memory of justice to fade.' After lecturing him I sentenced him. He accepted the sentence without murmur and his escort marched him away. I remember the uneasy shame I felt on days like that. I would leave the court-room and return to my apartment and sit in the rocking-chair in the dark all evening, without appetite, until it was time to go to bed. 'When some men suffer unjustly,' I said to myself, 'it is the fate of those who witness their suffering to suffer the shame of it.' But the specious consolation of this thought could not comfort me. I toyed more than once with the idea of resigning my post, retiring from public life, buying a small market garden. But then, I thought, someone else will be appointed to bear the shame of office, and nothing will have changed. So I continued in my duties until one day events overtook me.

The two horsemen are less than a mile away and already beginning to cross the bare fields by the time they are spied. I am one of the crowd that, hearing shouts from the walls, pours out in welcome; for we all recognize the green and gold battalion standard they bear. Among scampering excited children I stride across the freshly turned clods.

The horseman on the left, who has been riding shoulder to shoulder with his companion, turns away and trots off towards the lakeside track.

The other one continues to amble towards us, sitting very erect in the saddle, holding out his arms from his sides as if intending to embrace us or to fly up into the sky.

I begin to run as fast as I can, my sandals dragging in the earth, my heart pounding.

A hundred yards from him there is a thud of hooves behind and three armoured soldiers gallop past, racing towards the reed-brakes into which the other horseman has now disappeared.

I join the circle around the man (I recognize him, despite the change) who, with the standard flapping bravely above his head, gazes blankly towards the town. He is lashed to a stout wooden framework which holds him upright in his saddle. His spine is kept erect by a pole and his arms are tied to a cross-piece. Flies buzz around his face. His jaw is bound shut, his flesh is puffy, a sickly smell comes from him, he has been several days dead.

A child tugs at my hand. 'Is he a barbarian, uncle?' he whispers. 'No,' I whisper back. He turns to the boy next to him. 'You see, I told you,' he whispers.

Since no one else seems prepared to do it, I am the one to whose lot it falls to pick up the trailing reins and lead these tidings from the barbarians back through the great gates, past the silent watchers, to the barracks yard, there to cut their bearer loose and lay him out for burial.

The soldiers who set out after his lone companion are soon back. They canter across the square to the courthouse from which Mandel conducts his reign and disappear inside. When they reappear they will speak to no one.

Every premonition of disaster is confirmed, and for the first time true panic overtakes the town. The shops are swamped with customers bidding against each other for stocks of food. Some families barricade themselves in their houses, herding poultry and even pigs indoors with them. The school is closed. The rumour that a horde of barbarians is camped a few miles away on the charred river-banks, that an assault on the town is imminent, flashes from street corner to street corner. The unthinkable has occurred: the army that marched forth so gaily three months ago will never return.

The great gates are closed and barred. I plead with the sergeant of the watch to allow the fisherfolk inside. 'They are in terror of their lives,' I say. He turns his back on me without reply. Above our heads on the ramparts the soldiers, the forty men who stand between us and annihilation, gaze out over lake and desert.

At nightfall, on my way to the granary shed where I still sleep, I find my way blocked. A file of two-wheeled horse-drawn commissariat carts passes along the alley, the first loaded with what I recognize as sacks of seed grain from the granary, the others empty. They are followed by a file of horses, saddled and blanketed, from the garrison stables: every horse, I would guess, that has been stolen or commandeered in the past weeks. Roused by the noise, people emerge from their houses and stand quietly by watching this evidently long-planned manoeuvre of withdrawal.

I ask for an interview with Mandel, but the guard at the courthouse is as wooden as all his comrades.

In fact Mandel is not in the courthouse. I return to the square in time to hear the end of a statement he reads to the public 'in the name of the Imperial Command'. The withdrawal, he says, is a 'temporary measure'. A 'caretaker force' will be left behind. There is expected to be 'a general cessation of operations along the front for the duration of the winter'. He himself hopes to be back in the spring, when the army will 'initiate a new offensive'. He wishes to thank everyone for the 'unforgettable hospitality' he has been shown.

While he speaks, standing in one of the empty carts flanked by soldiers holding torches, his men are returning with the fruits of their foraging. Two struggle to load a handsome cast-iron stove looted from an empty house. Another comes back smiling in triumph bearing a cock and a hen, the cock a magnificent black and gold creature. Their legs are bound, he grips them by the wings, their fierce bird-eyes glare. While someone holds open the door he stuffs them into the oven. The cart is piled high with sacks and kegs from a looted shop, even a small table and two chairs. They unfold a heavy red carpet, spread it over the load, lash it down. There is no protest from the people who stand watching this methodical act of betrayal, but I feel currents of helpless anger all about me.

The last cart is loaded. The gates are unbarred, the soldiers mount. At the head of the column I can hear someone arguing with Mandel. 'Just an hour or so,' he is saying: 'they can be ready in an hour.' 'No question of that,' replies Mandel, the wind carrying the rest of his words away. A soldier pushes me out of his path and escorts three heavily bundled women to the last cart. They clamber aboard and seat themselves, holding up their veils to their faces. One of them carries a little girl whom she perches on top of the load. Whips crack, the column begins to move, the horses straining, the cartwheels creaking. At the rear of the column come two men with sticks driving a flock of a dozen sheep. As the sheep pass the murmur in the crowd grows. A young man dashes out waving his arms and shouting: the sheep scatter into the dark, and with a roar the crowd closes in. Almost at once the first shots crack out. Running as fast as I can in the midst of scores of other screaming running people, I retain only a single image of this futile attack: a man grappling with one of the women in the last cart, tearing at her clothes, the child watching wide-eyed with her thumb in her mouth. Then the square is empty and dark again, the last cart trundles through the gates, the garrison is gone.

For the rest of the night the gates stand open and little family groups, most of them on foot and weighed down under heavy packs, hurry after the soldiers. And before dawn the fisherfolk slink back in, meeting with no resistance, bringing their sickly children and their pitiful possessions and their bundles of poles and reeds with which to begin all over again the task of home-building.

My old apartment stands open. Inside the air is musty. Nothing has been dusted for a long time. The display cases – the stones and eggs and artifacts from the desert ruins – are gone. The furniture in the front room has been pushed against the walls and the carpet removed. The little parlour seems not to have been touched, but all the drapery carries a sour stuffy smell.

In the bedroom the bedclothes have been tossed aside with the same motion I use, as if I myself had been sleeping here. The odour from the unwashed linen is alien.

The chamber pot under the bed is half full. In the cupboard there is a crumpled shirt with a ring of brown inside the collar and yellow stains under the armpits. All my clothes are gone.

I strip the bed and lie down on the bare mattress, expecting some sense of unease to creep over me, the ghost of another man lingering still among his odours and disorders. The feeling does not come; the room is as familiar as ever. With my arm over my face I find myself drifting toward sleep. It may be true that the world as it stands is no illusion, no evil dream of a night. It may be that we wake up to it ineluctably, that we can neither forget it nor dispense with it. But I find it as hard as ever to believe that the end is near. If the barbarians were to burst in now, I know, I would die in my bed as stupid and ignorant as a baby. And even more apposite would it be if I were caught in the pantry downstairs with a spoon in my hand and my mouth full of fig preserve filched from the last bottle on the shelf: then my head could be hacked off and tossed on to the pile of heads on the square outside still wearing a look of hurt and guilty surprise at this irruption of history into the static time of the oasis. To each his own most fitting end. Some will be caught in dugouts beneath their cellars clutching their valuables to their breasts, pinching their eyes shut. Some will die on the road overwhelmed by the first snows of winter. Some few may even die fighting with pitchforks. After which the barbarians will wipe their backsides on the town archives. To the last we will have learned nothing. In all of us, deep down, there seems to be something granite and unteachable. No one truly believes, despite the hysteria in the streets, that the world of tranquil certainties we were born into is about to be extinguished. No one can accept that an Imperial army has been annihilated by men with bows and arrows and rusty old guns who live in tents and never wash and cannot read or write. And who am I to jeer at life-giving illusions? Is there any better way to pass these last days than in dreaming of a saviour with a sword who will scatter the enemy hosts and forgive us the errors that have been committed by others in our name and grant us a second chance to build our earthly paradise? I lie on the bare mattress and concentrate on bringing into life the image of myself as a swimmer swimming with even, untiring strokes through the medium of time, a medium more inert than water, without ripples, pervasive, colourless, odourless, dry as paper.

VI

Sometimes in the mornings there are fresh hoofprints in the fields. Among the straggling bushes that mark the far limit of the ploughed land the watchman sees a shape which he swears was not there the day before and which has vanished a day later. The fisherfolk will not venture out before sunrise. Their catch has dropped so low that they barely subsist.

In two days of co-operative effort in which we laboured with our weapons at our sides, we have harvested the far fields, all that was left after the flooding. The yield is less than four cups a day for each family, but better than nothing.

Although the blind horse continues to turn the wheel that fills the tank by the lakeshore that irrigates the gardens of the town, we know that the pipe can be cut at any time and have already begun with the digging of new wells within the walls.

I have urged my fellow-citizens to cultivate their kitchen gardens, to plant root vegetables that will withstand the winter frosts. 'Above all we must find ways of surviving the winter,' I tell them. 'In the spring they will send relief, there is no doubt of that. After the first thaw we can plant sixty-day millet.'

The school has been closed and the children are employed in trawling the salty southern fingers of the lake for the tiny red crustaceans that abound in the shallows. These we smoke and pack in one-pound slabs. They have a vile oily taste; normally only the fisherfolk eat them; but before the winter is out I suspect we will all be happy to have rats and insects to devour.

Along the north rampart we have propped a row of helmets with spears upright beside them. Every half-hour a child passes along the row moving each helmet slightly. Thus do we hope to deceive the keen eyes of the barbarians.

The garrison that Mandel bequeathed us consists of three men. They take turns in standing guard at the locked court-house door, ignored by the rest of the town, keeping to themselves.

In all measures for our preservation I have taken the lead. No one has challenged me. My beard is trimmed, I wear clean clothes, I have in effect resumed the legal administration that was interrupted a year ago by the arrival of the Civil Guard.

We ought to be cutting and storing firewood; but no one can be found who will venture into the charred woods along the river, where the fisherfolk swear they have seen fresh signs of barbarian encampments.

I am woken by a pounding on the door of my apartment. It is a man with a lantern, windburnt, gaunt, out of breath, in a soldier's greatcoat too large for him. He stares at me in bewil-derment.

'Who are you?' I say

'Where is the Warrant Officer?' he replies, panting, trying to look over my shoulder.

It is two o'clock in the morning. The gates have been opened to let in Colonel Joll's carriage, which stands with its shaft resting on the ground in the middle of the square. Several men shelter in its lee against the bitter wind. From the wall the men of the watch peer down.

'We need food, fresh horses, fodder,' my visitor is saying. He trots ahead of me, opens the door of the carriage, speaks: 'The Warrant Officer is not here, sir, he has left.' At the window, in the moonlight, I catch a glimpse of Joll himself. He sees me too: the door is slammed shut, I hear the click of the bolt inside. Peering through the glass I can make him out sitting in the dim far corner, rigidly averting his face. I rap on the glass but he pays no attention. Then his underlings shoulder me away.

Thrown out of the darkness, a stone lands on the roof of the carriage.

Another of Joll's escort comes running up. 'There is nothing,' he pants. 'The stables are empty, they have taken every single one.' The man who has unharnessed the sweating horses begins to curse. A second stone misses the carriage and nearly hits me. They are being thrown from the walls.

'Listen to me,' I say. 'You are cold and tired. Stable the horses, come inside, have something to eat, tell us your story. We have had no news since you left. If that madman wants to sit in his carriage all night, let him sit.'

They barely listen to me: famished, exhausted men who have done more than their duty in hauling this policeman to safety out of the clutches of the barbarians, they whisper together, already re-harnessing a pair of their weary horses.

I stare through the window at the faint blur against the blackness that is Colonel Joll. My cloak flaps, I shiver from the cold, but also from the tension of suppressed anger. An urge runs through me to smash the glass, to reach in and drag the man out through the jagged hole, to feel his flesh catch and tear on the edges, to hurl him to the ground and kick his body to pulp.

As though touched by this murderous current he reluctantly turns his face towards me. Then he sidles across the seat until he is looking at me through the glass. His face is naked, washed clean, perhaps by the blue moonlight, perhaps by physical exhaustion. I stare at his pale high temples. Memories of his mother's soft breast, of the tug in his hand of the first kite he ever flew, as well as of those intimate cruelties for which I abhor him, shelter in that beehive.

He looks out at me, his eyes searching my face. The dark lenses are gone. Must he too suppress an urge to reach out, claw me, blind me with splinters?

I have a lesson for him that I have long meditated. I mouth the words and watch him read them on my lips: 'The crime that is latent in us we must inflict on ourselves,' I say. I nod and nod, driving the message home. 'Not on others,' I say: I repeat the words, pointing at my chest, pointing at his. He watches my lips, his thin lips move in imitation, or perhaps in derision, I do not know. Another stone, heavier, perhaps a brick, hits the carriage with a thunderous clatter. He starts, the horses jerk in their traces.

Someone comes running up. 'Go!' he shouts. He pushes past me, beats at the door of the carriage. His arms are full of loaves. 'We must go!' he shouts. Colonel Joll slips the bolt and he tumbles the loaves in. The door slams shut. 'Hurry!' he shouts. The carriage heaves into motion, its springs groaning.

I grip the man's arm. 'Wait!' I cry. 'I will not let you go until I know what has happened!'

'Can't you see?' he shouts, beating at my grasp. My hands are still weak; to hold him I have to clasp him in a hug. 'Tell me and you can go!' I pant.

The carriage is nearing the gates. The two mounted men have already passed through; the other men run behind. Stones clatter against the carriage out of the darkness, shouts and curses rain down.

'What do you want to know?' he says, struggling vainly.

'Where is everyone else?'

'Gone. Scattered. All over the place. I don't know where they are. We had to find our own way. It was impossible to keep together.' As his comrades disappear into the night he wrestles harder. 'Let me go!' he sobs. He is no stronger than a child.

'In a minute. How could it be that the barbarians did this to you?'

'We froze in the mountains! We starved in the desert! Why did no one tell us it would be like that? We were not beaten – they led us out into the desert and then they vanished!'

'Who led you?'

'They – the barbarians! They lured us on and on, we could never catch them. They picked off the stragglers, they cut our horses loose in the night, they would not stand up to us!'

'So you gave up and came home?'

'Yes!'

'Do you expect me to believe that?'

He glares desperately back at me. 'Why should I lie?' he shouts. 'I don't want to be left behind, that is all!' He tears himself loose. Shielding his head with his hands, he races through the gate and into the darkness.

Digging has ceased at the third well-site. Some of the diggers have already gone home, others stand around waiting for orders.

'What is the trouble?' I say.

They point to the bones lying on a heap of fresh earth: a child's bones.

'There must have been a grave here,' I say. 'A strange place for a grave.' We are on the vacant plot behind the barracks, between the barracks and the south wall. The bones are old, they have absorbed the colour of the red clay. 'What do you want to do? We can start digging again nearer the wall if you like.'

They help me to climb into the pit. Standing chest-deep I scratch away the earth around the side of a jawbone embedded in the wall. 'Here is the skull,' I say. But no, the skull has already been dug up, they show it to me.

'Look under your feet,' says the foreman.

It is too dark to see, but when I chop lightly with the mattock I strike something hard; my fingers tell me it is bone.

'They aren't buried properly,' he says. He squats at the lip of the pit. 'They are lying just any old how, on top of each other.'

'Yes,' I say. 'We can't dig here, can we?'

'No,' he says.

'We must fill it in and start again nearer the wall.'

He is silent. He reaches out a hand and helps me clamber out. The bystanders say nothing either. I have to toss the bones back in and shovel the first earth before they will pick up their spades.

In the dream I stand again in the pit. The earth is damp, dark water seeps up, my feet squelch, it costs me a slow effort to lift them.

I feel under the surface, searching for the bones. My hand comes up with the corner of a jute sack, black, rotten, which crumbles away between my fingers. I dip back into the ooze. A fork, bent and tarnished. A dead bird, a parrot: I hold it by the tail, its bedraggled feathers hang down, its soggy wings droop, its eye sockets are empty. When I release it, it falls through the surface without a splash. 'Poisoned water,' I think. 'I must be careful not to drink here. I must not touch my right hand to my mouth.'

I have not slept with a woman since I returned from the desert. Now at this most inappropriate of times my sex begins to reassert itself. I sleep badly and wake up in the mornings with a sullen erection growing like a branch out of my groin. It has nothing to do with desire. Lying in my rumpled bed I wait in vain for it go away. I try to invoke images of the girl who night after night slept here with me. I see her standing barelegged in her shift, one foot in the basin, waiting for me to wash her, her hand pressing down on my shoulder. I lather the stocky calf. She slips the shift up over her head. I lather her thighs; then I put the soap aside, embrace her hips, rub my face in her belly. I can smell the soap, feel the warmth of the water, the pressure of her hands. From the depths of that memory I reach out to touch myself. There is no leap of response. It is like touching my own wrist: part of myself, but hard, dull, a limb with no life of its own. I try to bring it off: futile, for there is no feeling. 'I am tired,' I tell myself.

For an hour I sit in an armchair waiting for this rod of blood to dwindle. In its own good time it does. Then I dress and go out.

In the night it comes back: an arrow growing out of me, pointing nowhere. Again I try to feed it on images, but detect no answering life.

'Try bread mould and milkroot,' the herbalist says. 'It may

work. If it does not, come back to me. Here is some milkroot. You grind it and mix it to a paste with the mould and a little warm water. Take two spoonfuls after each meal. It is very unpleasant, very bitter, but be assured it will not do you any harm.'

I pay him in silver. No one but children will take copper coins any more.

'But tell me,' he says: 'why should a fine healthy man like yourself want to kill off his desires?'

'It has nothing to do with desire, father. It is simply an irritation. A stiffening. Like rheumatism.'

He smiles. I smile back.

'This must be the only shop in town they did not loot,' I say. It is not a shop, just a recess and a front under an awning, with racks of dusty jars and, hanging from hooks on the wall, roots and bunches of dried leaves, the medicines with which he has dosed the town for fifty years.

'Yes, they did not trouble me. They suggested that I leave for my own good. "The barbarians will fry your balls and eat them" – that was what they said, those were their words. I said, "I was born here, I'll die here, I'm not leaving." Now they are gone, and it's better without them, I say.'

'Yes.'

'Try the milkroot. If it doesn't work, come back.'

I drink the bitter concoction and eat as much lettuce as I can, since people say that lettuce takes away one's potency. But I do all this half-heartedly, aware that I am misinterpreting the signs.

I also call on Mai. The inn had closed down, there being too little custom; now she comes in to help her mother in the barracks. I find her in the kitchen putting her baby to sleep in its cot near the stove. 'I love the big old stove you have here,' she says. 'It keeps its warmth for hours. Such a gentle warmth.' She brews tea; we sit at the table watching the glowing coals through the grate. 'I wish I had something nice to offer you,' she says, 'but the soldiers cleaned out the storeroom, there is hardly anything left.'

'I want you to come upstairs with me,' I say. 'Can you leave the child here?'

We are old friends. Years ago, before she married the second time, she used to visit me in my apartment in the afternoons.

'I'd rather not leave him,' she says, 'in case he wakes up alone.' So I wait while she wraps the child, and then follow her up the stairs: a young woman still, with a heavy body and shapeless spreading thighs. I try to recall what it was like with her, but cannot. In those days all women pleased me.

She settles the child on cushions in a corner, murmuring to it till it falls asleep again.

'It is just for a night or two,' I say. 'Everything is coming to an end. We must live as we can.' She drops her drawers, trampling on them like a horse, and comes to me in her smock. I blow out the lamp. My words have left me dispirited.

As I enter her she sighs. I rub my cheek against hers. My hand finds her breast; her own hand closes over it, caresses it, pushes it aside. 'I am a bit sore,' she whispers. 'From the baby.'

I am still searching for something I want to say when I feel the climax come, far-off, slight, like an earth-tremor in another part of the world.

'This is your fourth child, isn't it?' We lie side by side under the covers.

'Yes, the fourth. One died.'

'And the father? Does he help?'

'He left some money behind. He was with the army.'

'I am sure he will come back.'

I feel her placid weight against my side. 'I have grown very fond of your eldest boy,' I say. 'He used to bring me my meals while I was locked up.' We lie for a while in silence. Then my head begins to spin. I re-emerge from sleep in time to hear the tail-end of a rattle from my throat, an old man's snore.

She sits up. 'I will have to go,' she says. 'I can't sleep in such bare rooms, I hear creaking all night.' I watch her dim shape move as she dresses and picks up the child. 'Can I light the lamp?' she says. 'I'm afraid of falling on the stairs. Go to sleep.

I will bring you breakfast in the morning, if you don't mind millet porridge.'

'I liked her very much,' she says. 'We all did. She never complained, she always did what she was asked, though I know her feet gave her pain. She was friendly. There was always something to laugh about when she was around.'

Again I am as dull as wood. She labours with me: her big hands stroke my back, grip my buttocks. The climax comes: like a spark struck far away over the sea and lost at once.

The baby begins to whimper. She eases herself away from me and gets up. Big and naked, she walks back and forth across the patch of moonlight with the baby over her shoulder, patting it, crooning. 'He will be asleep in a minute,' she whispers. I am half asleep myself when I feel her cool body settle down again beside me, her lips nuzzle my arm.

'I don't want to think about the barbarians,' she says. 'Life is too short to spend worrying about the future.'

I have nothing to say.

'I don't make you happy,' she says. 'I know you don't enjoy it with me. You are always somewhere else.'

I wait for her next words.

'She told me the same thing. She said you were somewhere else. She could not understand you. She did not know what you wanted from her.'

'I didn't know you and she were intimate.'

'I was often here, downstairs. We talked to each other about what was on our minds. Sometimes she would cry and cry and cry. You made her very unhappy. Did you know that?'

She is opening a door through which a wind of utter desolation blows on me.

'You don't understand,' I say huskily. She shrugs. I go on: 'There is a whole side to the story you don't know, that she could not have told you because she did not know it herself. Which I don't want to talk about now.'

'It is none of my business.'

We are silent, thinking our own thoughts about the girl who tonight sleeps far away under the stars.

'Perhaps when the barbarians come riding in,' I say, 'she will come riding with them.' I imagine her trotting through the open gateway at the head of a troop of horsemen, erect in the saddle, her eyes shining, a forerunner, a guide, pointing out to her comrades the lay of this foreign town where she once lived. 'Then everything will be on a new footing.'

We lie in the dark thinking.

'I am terrified,' she says. 'I am terrified to think what is going to become of us. I try to hope for the best and live from day to day. But sometimes all of a sudden I find myself imagining what might happen and I am paralyzed with fear. I don't know what to do any more. I can only think of the children. What is going to become of the children?' She sits up in the bed. *'What is going to become of the children?'* she demands vehemently.

'They won't harm the children,' I tell her. 'They won't harm anyone.' I stroke her hair, calm her, hold her tight, till it is time again to feed the baby.

She sleeps better downstairs in the kitchen, she says. She feels more secure when she can wake up and see the glow of coals in the grate. Also she likes to have the child with her in the bed. Also it is better if her mother does not find out where she spends the nights.

I too feel it was a mistake and do not visit her again. Sleeping alone, I miss the scent of thyme and onion on her fingertips. For an evening or two I experience a quiet, fickle sadness, before I begin to forget.

I stand out in the open watching the coming of the storm. The sky has been fading till now it is bone-white with tones of pink rippling in the north. The ochre rooftiles glisten, the air grows luminous, the town shines out shadowless, mysteriously beautiful in these last moments.

I climb the wall. Among the armed dummies stand people staring out towards the horizon where a great cloud of dust and sand already boils up. No one speaks.

The sun turns coppery. The boats have all left the lake, the birds have stopped singing. There is an interval of utter silence. Then the wind strikes.

In the shelter of our homes, with the windows bolted and bolsters pushed against the doors, with fine grey dust already sifting through roof and ceiling to settle on every uncovered surface, film the drinking water, grate on our teeth, we sit thinking of our fellow-creatures out in the open who at times like this have no recourse but to turn their backs to the wind and endure.

In the evenings, in the hour or two I can afford at the fireplace before my ration of wood gives out and I must creep into bed, I occupy myself in my old hobbies, repairing as best I can the cases of stones I found smashed and tossed away in the courthouse gardens, toying again with the decipherment of the archaic writing on the poplar slips.

It seems right that, as a gesture to the people who inhabited the ruins in the desert, we too ought to set down a record of settlement to be left for posterity buried under the walls of our town; and to write such a history no one would seem to be better fitted than our last magistrate. But when I sit down at my writing-table, wrapped against the cold in my great old bearskin, with a single candle (for tallow too is rationed) and a pile of yellowed documents at my elbow, what I find myself beginning to write is not the annals of an Imperial outpost or an account of how the people of that outpost spent their last year composing their souls as they waited for the barbarians.

'No one who paid a visit to this oasis,' I write, 'failed to be struck by the charm of life here. We lived in the time of the seasons, of the harvests, of the migrations of the waterbirds. We lived with nothing between us and the stars. We would have made any concession, had we only known what, to go on living here. This was paradise on earth.'

For a long while I stare at the plea I have written. It would be disappointing to know that the poplar slips I have spent so much time on contain a message as devious, as equivocal, as reprehensible as this.

'Perhaps by the end of the winter,' I think, 'when hunger truly bites us, when we are cold and starving, or when the barbarian is truly at the gate, perhaps then I will abandon the locutions of a civil servant with literary ambitions and begin to tell the truth.'

I think: 'I wanted to live outside history. I wanted to live outside the history that Empire imposes on its subjects, even its lost subjects. I never wished it for the barbarians that they should have the history of Empire laid upon them. How can I believe that that is cause for shame?'

I think: 'I have lived through an eventful year, yet understand no more of it than a babe in arms. Of all the people of this town I am the one least fitted to write a memorial. Better the blacksmith with his cries of rage and woe.'

I think: 'But when the barbarians taste bread, new bread and mulberry jam, bread and gooseberry jam, they will be won over to our ways. They will find that they are unable to live without the skills of men who know how to rear the pacific grains, without the arts of women who know how to use the benign fruits.'

I think: 'When one day people come scratching around in the ruins, they will be more interested in the relics from the desert than in anything I may leave behind. And rightly so.' (Thus I spend an evening coating the slips one by one in linseed oil and wrapping them in an oilcloth. When the wind lets up, I promise myself, I will go out and bury them where I found them.)

I think: 'There has been something staring me in the face, and still I do not see it.'

The wind has dropped, and now the snowflakes come floating down, the first fall of the year, flecking the rooftiles with white. All morning I stand at my window watching the snow fall. When I cross the barracks yard it is already inches deep and my footsteps crunch with an eerie lightness.

In the middle of the square there are children at play building a snowman. Anxious not to alarm them, but inexplicably joyful, I approach them across the snow.

They are not alarmed, they are too busy to cast me a glance. They have completed the great round body, now they are rolling a ball for the head.

'Someone fetch things for the mouth and nose and eyes,' says the child who is their leader.

It strikes me that the snowman will need arms too, but I do not want to interfere.

They settle the head on the shoulders and fill it out with pebbles for eyes, ears, nose and mouth. One of them crowns it with his cap.

It is not a bad snowman.

This is not the scene I dreamed of. Like much else nowadays I leave it feeling stupid, like a man who lost his way long ago but presses on along a road that may lead nowhere.